MODERN WORLD NATIONS

Croatia

Zoran Pavlović

Series Consulting Editor
Charles F. Gritzner
South Dakota State University

CHELSEA HOUSE
PUBLISHERS
A Haights Cross Communications Company

Philadelphia

Frontispiece: Flag of Croatia

Cover: Dubrovnik, Croatia.

CHELSEA HOUSE PUBLISHERS

VP, NEW PRODUCT DEVELOPMENT Sally Cheney
DIRECTOR OF PRODUCTION Kim Shinners
CREATIVE MANAGER Takeshi Takahashi
MANUFACTURING MANAGER Diann Grasse

Staff for CROATIA

EDITOR Lee Marcott
PRODUCTION EDITOR Jaimie Winkler
PICTURE RESEARCHER Sarah Bloom
COVER AND SERIES DESIGNER Takeshi Takahashi
LAYOUT 21st Century Publishing and Communications, Inc.

A Haights Cross Communications Company

http://www.chelseahouse.com

First Printing

1 3 5 7 9 8 6 4 2

Library of Congress Cataloging-in-Publication Data

Pavlovic, Zoran.
   Croatia/Zoran Pavlovic.
      p. cm. —(Modern world nations)
Includes index.
   ISBN 0-7910-7210-X
   1. Croatia—Juvenile literature. I. Title. II. Series.
DR1510 .P38 2002
949.72—dc21

                                                                2002011526

Table of Contents

Croatia

Throughout its history, Croatians have been attracted to the sea. Today, the lure of the Adriatic continues to draw thousands of tourists to the coastal region with its many natural land cultural attractions.

Introducing Croatia

A map of Europe looks much different today than it did just a decade or two ago. In the late 1980s, Europe was divided into two political spheres—the democratic West and the Soviet-dominated East. Only a few countries were neutral in this Cold War, or ideological conflict, between Eastern and Western Europe. Today, the Soviet Union no longer exists. Neither does the former Soviet-era country of Yugoslavia. Nearly 20 new countries have risen from the ashes of their remains. Croatia is one of these newly independent states. As one of the six former Yugoslavia's socialist republics, Croatia gained its independence after the fall of Communism.

Many people place Croatia in the western part of a region identified as the Balkan Peninsula. But this is a misconception. The "Balkan Peninsula" is not a correct geographical term. Rather, it is the product of gross misunderstanding by historians, political scientists, the media, and others who fail to fully grasp the region's many and complex geographical differences. Such mistakes may seem trivial. But if unchallenged, they can contribute to a flawed understanding of the region and its people. This is particularly true when all people living from southern Greece to Slovenia and northern Croatia are placed under the same "Balkans" roof.

Geographically, the Balkan region is not a peninsula; it is a mountain range located primarily in Bulgaria. Peninsulas, after all, are areas of land surrounded on three sides by water. On a map, it is clear that the land occupied by Croatia does not fit this definition. Because of the great historical, cultural, and ethnic diversity of the people in this part of southeastern Europe, it is a serious mistake to place them all in one group. Croatians, for example, take great pride in what they believe to be their many unique cultural traits.

Croatia is located in southeastern Europe. Its people and their way of life represent a blend of Mediterranean and Danube cultures. Even though Croatia's cultural heritage is one of the richest and oldest in Europe, it actually is a young country. Croatia became independent in 1991, after centuries of struggle for independence. That struggle, among other reasons, contributed to a large wave of emigration (people leaving) from the country during the 20th century. Today, Croatians occupy a country that is about the size of West Virginia. But they are also proud to be citizens of many lands throughout the world.

Croats call their homeland *Hrvatska*, which means "the land of Croats" in their native tongue. But no one is sure about the origins of the name Hrvat (Croat). Legend says that five brothers—Kloukas, Lobelos, Kosentzes, Mouhlo, and Hrobatos—together with their two sisters, Touga and Bouga, were leaders of the Croatian tribes in ancient times. From one of the brothers, Hrobatos, they believe, the name was later used to mark all members of the Croatian nation.

This book will take a reading tour of Croatia. It will wander through its past and present and take a glimpse into its future. The

Croatia is one of the six former Yugoslavia's socialist republics, which gained its independence in 1991 after the fall of Communism. It is about the size of West Virginia and is located in southeastern Europe. Croatia has a long coastline and is blessed with a very mild and pleasant Mediterranean climate.

next chapters will highlight the country's unique physical landscapes, discuss many of its people, and explore its government and economic activity. The journey will travel through many of Croatia's cities and regions, each of which offers something special.

The town of Trogir is located on the south Adriatic coast and is a tourist destination because of its waterways and architecture. The portal of the cathedral in Trogir is an example of 13th-century Dalmatian masonry.

Physical Environment

In terms of its natural environment, Croatia is a tourist's dream come true. The country shares many similarities with California. Both are blessed with a very mild and pleasant Mediterranean climate. They both have long coastlines that rank among the world's most scenic. Each location has varied terrain, contributing to diverse landscapes and ecosystems.

Unlike California, however, Croatia has hundreds of coastal bays, inlets, and coves. Offshore, more than 1,000 islands of varying sizes rise above the sparkling clear blue water of the Adriatic Sea. As in California, immediately inland from the coast, the land becomes more rugged. In Croatia, however, the low, yet scenic, mountains offer the traveler some of the world's finest and most extensive examples of karst topography (landforms). Water, wearing away soft rock over thousands of years, has created an array of unique landform features.

They include strange looking plateaus, valleys and hills, sink-holes, and rugged surfaces. There are also underground lakes and streams. But the best-known features in karst regions are caves. Croatia boasts of having more than 8,000 caverns, many of which have not yet been fully explored—the country is a spelunker's (a person who explores caves) paradise.

Still further east, the land flattens out to create fertile plains that produce most of Croatia's crops. Finally, scattered about the country are a number of national parks and other preserved environments that offer glimpses of unique landforms, ecosystems, animal life, and other geographic features.

Location

Look at the map of Croatia and use some imagination—doesn't the country's shape resemble the head of a huge (1,067 square miles; 2,763 square kilometers), eastward-facing alligator with its jaws opened wide? Within its gaping mouth is neighboring Bosnia and Herzegovina. Its long chin rests on the coast of the Adriatic Sea—a narrow extension of the Mediterranean Sea that separates Croatia from Italy, its neighbor to the west. The top of its head bumps up against its northern neighbors, Slovenia and Hungary. Finally, the tip of its snout is poking into northern Yugoslavia.

Location is perhaps the most important of all geographic concepts. And in this regard, Croatia is both blessed and cursed. It is blessed by occupying one of the world's most beautiful and unique landscapes. Also, it is situated in an ideal crossroads setting between the Mediterranean Sea and central Europe. To the south lie the historical treasures of the Mediterranean—Greece, Italy, and lands beyond. To the north are the heavily populated industrial countries of Europe. Today, as in the past, many important trade routes pass through Croatia. By vehicle, much of central Europe can be reached in an easy day's drive.

Croatia's location has also been a curse in some respects. The

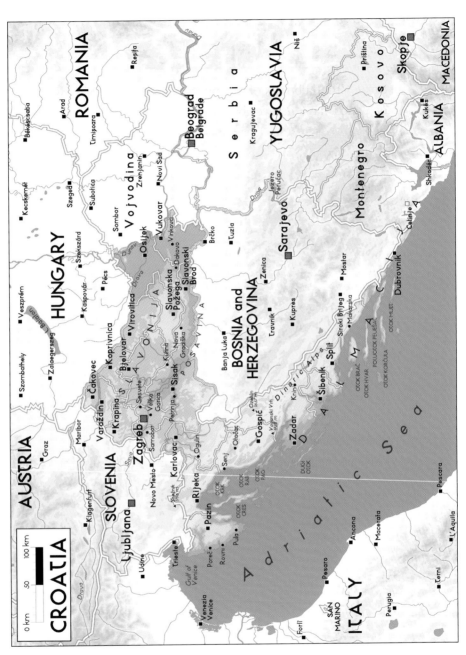

From its narrow Adriatic coastal plain and its high and rugged western mountains, Croatia gradually drops in elevation to broad, fertile plains in the north and east. Geographers divide the country into three regions: the Adriatic coast, the interior highlands, and the eastern lowland plains.

Balkan region has long been one of Europe's most troubled areas. It is an area in which deep ethnic hatreds have smoldered for centuries and often have broken into searing conflicts that have torn countries, ethnic groups, and even families apart. During much of the 20th century, the region also fell behind the Iron Curtain—under the heavy fist of Communist control. Many of today's political, economic, social, and ethnic problems that plague the region can be traced to the influences imposed during this period. These influences will be discussed in greater detail in Chapter 4, "Government and Economy."

The Land

From its narrow Adriatic coastal plain and its high and rugged western mountains, Croatia gradually drops in elevation to broad, fertile plains in the north and east. Geographers have divided the country into three general landform regions: the Adriatic coast, the interior highlands, and the eastern lowland plains. Each environment has different characteristics and different land use practices and potentials. The journey begins along the beautiful shore of the Adriatic Sea and works its way eastward through each of the regions.

Adriatic Coast

Croatia's coast is judged by many people to be one of the world's most beautiful shorelines. It stretches the entire length of the country's western, or Adriatic, border. Here, however, is a wonderful example of why it is necessary to exercise caution when interpreting statistical data. According to most sources, Croatia's coast extends for more than 1,100 miles (1,770 kilometers) along the Adriatic. Yet by taking a close look at a map and by using the distance scale, the distance from the northern to southern tip of the country, along the coast, is only about 300 miles (483 kilometers). The difference between the two distances provides the first glimpse of the nature of this coast—it is one of the most jagged in the world. In fact, only Norway, with its many fjords (long glacially scoured "arms" of the sea that reach far inland), has a more indented coastline.

Many islands—an estimated 1,185 of them—lie scattered about the waters off Croatia's Adriatic coast. Sixty-six of the islands are inhabited; others include various-sized islets, rocks, and reefs peaking above sea level. All of them, regardless of size, help to create yet another 2,500 miles (4,023 kilometers) of coastline. The largest islands are Krk and Cres. Both are located in the north, in Kvarner Bay, a shallow thumb of the Adriatic Sea tucked between the Istrian Peninsula and the mainland. The island of Cres is noted for a rather unique physical feature—there is a freshwater lake on the island. Jubuka, an island located nearly 60 miles off the southern Croatian coast, is volcanic. From the distance, it appears on the horizon like a black pyramid, with slopes plunging almost vertically into the sea.

The southern coastal region, called Dalmatia, is more rugged than in the north. Here, the Dinaric Alps plunge to the coast, leaving a narrow strip of rugged land with little flat terrain. The region is somewhat remote and also quite barren. But the combination of sea, islands, and mountain slopes makes this one of the country's most scenic regions. It also is a region that offers great potential for future economic development, particularly for tourism.

Interior Highlands

Immediately inland from the coast, the land becomes quite rugged and is less developed. Here, several parallel ranges of mountains form the Dinaric Alps. The area is often called Croatia's Switzerland. But the Dinarics are no match for the towering, snow-capped alpine ranges farther west, which stretch from eastern France into Austria. Much of the region lies at elevations of between 1,000 and 2,000 feet. And even the highest peaks reach only about 6,000 feet—somewhat lower than the higher Appalachian peaks in the eastern United States, or South Dakota's Black Hills. This region offers great potential

The Dinaric Alps in the Dalmatian region rise along the Adriatic coast. The mountains have large limestone areas, and the plateau areas are marked by caves, underground streams, and valleys due to the effects of erosion by groundwater.

for the development of winter tourism and various types of mountain recreation activities.

Eastern Lowland Plains

Much of eastern and northeastern Croatia is relatively low and flat, with the plains broken here and there by scattered hills and low mountains. The Drava and Sava rivers, both tributaries to the mighty Danube River, drain the region, known as the Pannonian Plains. In some areas, sluggish streams have created marshlands. But elsewhere, they have carried material eroded from their highland headwaters and deposited this material on the plains below. It is this alluvium (stream-deposited soil) that creates the rich soils that make this region Croatia's most important area of farming and livestock herding. It is also where most of the country's people live.

Climate and Ecosystems

Weather is the current atmospheric condition; climate is a many-year average of weather conditions. Ecosystems can be thought of as being the natural elements, or physical landscapes, that people actually "see" when traveling through climatic regions: the natural vegetation, the soils, the animal life, and the water features. Most of Croatia lies between 43 and 46 degrees north latitude, placing it at the same distance from the equator as Oregon and South Dakota. Yet because of its closeness to the Mediterranean Sea, its climate is much more like that of Oregon, than of South Dakota. It enjoys a relatively mild climate, one that lacks the extreme high and low temperatures of more interior locations. In the west, along the coast and in the western high-lands, both the climate and ecosystem are Mediterranean—similar to the environmental conditions that occur in California west of the Sierra Nevada. In the eastern lowland plains, climate is humid continental, with conditions similar to those found in Missouri. Mountains, of course, create their own climatic conditions. A 1,000-foot (305 meters) change in elevation can create the same change in temperature that one might experience in traveling through a 400-mile (644 kilometers) span of latitude.

Mediterranean Climate and Ecosystem

Generally speaking, temperatures are moderate along the coast. A dominant characteristic of the Mediterranean climate is its lack of extremes. It is also sunny much of the time—in fact, Croatia's Adriatic coast is one of the brightest in all of Europe, averaging 2,600 hours of sunlight yearly. Summers are warm, but not uncomfortably hot; winters, on the other hand, tend to be quite mild. The lack of extremes is explained by the sea's moderating effect on temperature. Water bodies do not get as hot, or as cold, as do adjacent landmasses. Therefore, temperatures on land bordering a large body of water tend to be more moderate than those occurring farther inland. The coastal city of Dubrovnik experiences a mild January temperature average of 48°F (9°C); frost and snow rarely occur. In July, the hottest month of the year, the temperature averages a pleasant 77°F (25°C), and scorching temperatures are almost unknown. Annual precipitation along the coast averages 25 inches (64 centimeters) to a maximum of 40 inches (102 centimeters). But the Mediterranean climate is unique in one important way—it is the only climatic region that experiences a prolonged period of summer aridity. Here, as in much of California, nearly all of the precipitation falls during the late fall, winter, and early spring months.

Winds are common to the coastal area. Sea-land breezes occur almost daily. During the day, coastal areas are cooled by sea breezes—winds blowing from the cooler sea over the warmer land. (Directional winds take the name of the direction *from* which they blow; therefore, a land breeze blows from land to sea, and a northeasterly wind blows from the northeast.) At night, direction changes as land-breezes blow from the interior toward the sea.

The strongest wind along the coast is the *bora*. It is a dry wind that can blow with very strong intensity from the north and northeast. During the winter, a bora can last as long as two weeks. It blows down from the mountains toward the sea, often howling through the passes and canyons. The strongest bora blows in the northern Adriatics, with average wind velocity gradually slowing down in southern Croatia. Along the entire Adriatic coast, however, these fierce winds can reach hurricane-strength proportions. They can cause tremendous damage to buildings and other structures, woodlands, and coasts.

The town of Senj, located at the western end of a mountain

pass a short drive south from the city of Rijeka, is often the victim of the bora. Even Croatian folklore and literature recognize Senj's fierce bora storms. The wind is particularly strong here because of Senj's unique location. The bora is caused when an intense low-pressure system forms to the west and a strong high pressure system forms to the east. Just as water flows from high elevation to low elevation, air blows from an area of high atmospheric pressure to one of low pressure. When air blows from east to west in this region, the high mountains block it—just as a dam stops a river's flow. Senj, however, is located at the western end of a mountain pass that serves as a funnel for the moving air. As the wind blasts from the mouth of the pass, it often stops traffic along much of the Croatian coast. Another wind affecting the coastal region is the sirocco. This is a warm, moist wind that blows mostly from the south, bringing with it high waves and rain.

The Mediterranean ecosystem is unlike any other in the world. It is adapted to two primary controls. First, the region receives ample moisture for plant growth, but it also experiences a severe and prolonged summer drought. For this reason, many plants go into their dormant period during the summer, rather than winter, months. Second, because of summer drought, all Mediterranean regions (including southern California) experience widespread and often severe wildfires during the summer and early autumn months. The vegetation has adapted to these conditions, and is pyrophytic (fire resistant), composed mainly of grass, shrubs, and scattered small trees. Valley alluvial (stream-deposited) soils are fertile, although seasonal drought makes irrigation necessary for most crops during summer months.

Mountainous Interior

Moving inland, into the Dinaric Alps and associated ranges, weather conditions change abruptly. Here, elevation and exposure (north- or south-facing slope, determining exposure to the sun) are the primary influences on weather and climate. On the Adriatic-facing slopes, conditions resemble those of

the lower coastal region to the west. In the mountains themselves, temperatures tend to be considerably lower (dropping by
about 3.5°F (-17°C) for each additional 1,000 feet (305 meters) of
elevation). During winter months, temperatures can plummet to
below freezing. Croatia's lowest recorded temperature is a bone-
chilling -13°F (-25°C). Mountainous regions receive the highest
amounts of precipitation to occur anywhere in the country,
receiving an average 80–120 inches (203–304 centimeters) per
year. Here, precipitation is more equally spread out through the
year, and heavy winter snow is common.

Mountain ecosystems also vary with local conditions of
weather and climate. At the same elevation on a hill, for example,
the north-facing slope can be densely forested, whereas just a few
miles away, on a south-facing slope, there is only sparse grass and
scrub vegetation. The difference is explained by exposure to the
sun. The south-facing slope receives more sunlight, hence it is
warmer; this, in turn, results in greater loss of moisture through
evaporation. Because of their relative lack of human settlement
and extensive economic development, much of the mountainous
environment remains forested. About 36 percent of Croatia is in
woodlands, most of which occurs in this region. Deciduous
woodlands predominate, with varieties of oak and beech being
most common. In places, however, forests suffer from widespread
air pollution (such as acid rain) and unwise deforestation. The
mountains also abound in wildlife. Large animals include bear,
deer, boar, wildcat, and wild sheep. There also are hare, fox, lynx,
and wolves. Many species of birds are also found in the region.

Northern and Eastern Humid Continental

This region is Croatia's population and economic heart-
land. Here, the climate is similar to that of the more humid
central interior of the United States. Summers are hot and
humid, and winters are cool to cold. Summer temperatures
have reached a sweltering 113°F (45°C); winter temperatures,
on the other hand, can plunge well below 32°F (0°C) and

occasionally below 0°F (-17°C). Zagreb, the capital and largest city, experiences a January temperature average of 32°F (0°C) and a July average of 75°F (24°C). These temperature conditions are almost identical to those throughout much of central and eastern Missouri. Originally, this region supported a dense cover of deciduous forest. However, thousands of years of human settlement, land clearing, and agriculture have destroyed nearly all of the original woodlands. Widespread marshlands also occur in some of the more poorly drained parts of the northern and eastern plains.

Water Features

Although the Adriatic coastal area of Croatia experiences prolonged and severe summer drought, nearly all of the country has adequate moisture for human settlement and economic development.

Croatia's major water feature is the Adriatic Sea. Because water in the Adriatic swirls in a counterclockwise direction, the sea has some of the cleanest water in the entire Mediterranean Sea (geographically, the Adriatic Sea is an extension, or part, of the Mediterranean). In places, objects on the bottom can be seen at a depth of more than 100 feet. The sea is rich in marine resources, including hundreds of edible fish and shellfish species.

Most of Croatia's rivers are in the east, where they flow from the surrounding mountains eastward into the Black Sea basin. Major rivers include the Sava, which flows from Slovenia southward, through Zagreb and across central Croatia, where it forms part of the southern boundary with Bosnia and Herzegovina before joining the Danube. The Drava River forms a large portion of Croatia's eastern boundary with Hungary and Yugoslavia. Even the mighty Danube touches a small part of the country's eastern tip. The west, you may recall, is a region of karst topography (limestone landforms). Whereas a few streams plunge down the western slopes of the Dinaric Mountains into the Adriatic, the region has few rivers. Karst is

Mountains rise abruptly from the Adriatic Sea along the Dalmatian Coast. This region is dominated by limestone rock and karst landforms.

associated with limestone rock, which is very porous—that is, water sinks into the rock very quickly. Here, as in parts of Indiana and Florida (states with large areas of limestone and karst topography), many of the streams are underground.

About 90 percent of all natural lakes in the world were created by glacial action. The land that is now Croatia was too far south and too low in elevation to have undergone extensive Ice Age glaciation. Therefore, it does not have many lakes. And of the lakes that it does have, none of them is large. Lake Vrana, located south of Zadar on the northern Dalmatian Coast, is the country's largest freshwater body. There are several small reservoirs—which are artificial lakes on rivers behind dams. Perhaps Croatia's best-known and most unique lake is Vrana, a freshwater body occupying a depression on the island of Cres. In the karst region, water seeping into the earth has eroded rock and formed huge caverns. Many caverns are dry, or partially dry, caves; others, however, are filled all or in part with water to form enormous underground lakes.

Croatia also has a number of thermal (warm water) springs, all of which are located in the interior areas of the country. Water in some of the springs also has a high mineral content. The combination of warm and mineral rich water supposedly has healing properties. Hence, a number of the springs have given rise to important spas that attract thousands of people seeking their curative powers.

Mineral Resources

Croatia has a variety of useful mineral resources. Before the outbreak of regional warfare in 1991, mining and quarrying were important contributors to the country's economy. Of greatest importance are its mineral fuels. There are good deposits of petroleum, natural gas, and coal. In peaceful times, the country has the energy resources needed to build a strong industrial base. Additionally, there is some iron ore, bauxite (the ore from which aluminum is made), and clay suited to the making of chinaware.

Environmental Hazards

Although much of Croatia is quite safe from natural hazards, the country does offer some environmental elements that can result in devastation. In addition to the damage caused by the bora and its howling winds, heavy rains can cause problems in the mountains. Flash floods can occur, resulting in torrents of water sweeping down steep mountainsides causing serious erosion and destroying everything in their path. Landslides and mudflows, also usually occurring after periods of heavy rain, also pose a threat in the mountains. On the lowland plains, heavy rain or rapid snowmelt can cause widespread local flooding. And in the Dinaric Alps, particularly around the city of Knin, earthquakes occur rather frequently.

The country's major environmental threat, however, is wildfire. In this context, it is important to remember that coastal Croatia is similar to coastal southern California. Each summer, hundreds of fires ravage southern California's landscape—often causing millions of dollars in damage. In the Mediterranean climate, vegetation thrives during the wet winter months, but during the parched summer months, it dries out, creating an environmental tinderbox. A simple spark can ignite a match-sized flicker of flame that can become a raging inferno in a matter of minutes. Heat generated by the flames can create its own firestorm. As air rushes in toward the fire, it creates a bellows affect. This not only fans the flames, but also the resulting winds can reach 100 miles (162 kilometers) per hour—causing the entire fire system to move at an alarming rate of speed. Until finally stopped, searing flames and heat often in excess of 1,000°F (378°C) will destroy anything in the fire's way. Here, as in California, humans acting in a reckless and thoughtless manner create nearly 100 percent of all such fires.

Preserving the Environment

Croatia has taken steps to preserve large portions of its rich natural heritage. In fact, today about 8 percent of the country is protected parkland. And there are plans to almost double the country's area devoted to environmental preservation to 15 percent—a figure that is matched by very few other nations.

The country takes great pride in its seven national parks. Three parks are in mountain regions and four are scattered along the Adriatic coast. Paklenica Park is in the Velebit, Croatia's largest mountain range (part of the Dinaric Alps). Deep gorges, unique land formations, dense woodlands, rare plant species, and abundant wildlife make this park a tourist's paradise. Risnjak Park is in the Gorski Kotar region, where it offers protection to the country's most densely wooded area. Plitvice National Park features 16 small lakes, connected by more than 90 waterfalls.

The coastal parks take advantage of the Adriatic region's natural beauty, including its freshwater, saltwater, many islands, vegetation and animal life, and distinctive karst landscapes. The National Park of Krka spotlights the Krka River as it cascades through deep canyons, creating lakes, waterfalls, and rapids as it plunges to the sea. Brijuni Park protects a group of 14 islands located offshore from Pula, at the tip of the Istrian Peninsula. The more than 100 islands that make up the Kornati Archipelago—the largest island group in the Mediterranean—are the site of Kornati Park. Marine life, towering cliffs, and rugged coastal features add to the beauty of the islands themselves. Finally, in the far south, near Dubrovnik, is the Mljet National Park. Here, two lakes are linked with both the sea and to each other by narrow, nearly hidden, passageways.

Additionally, there are a variety of other parks and protected areas. These include nature parks, various reserves, natural monuments, protected nature areas, parks-forests, and various areas protecting special plant and animal species.

Much of Croatia has a pleasant, varied, and scenic environment. The country does not suffer from extremes of temperature, and its entire area receives adequate moisture to support settlement and economic development. Whereas much of the country is hilly to mountainous, elevations are relatively low; hence, they do not pose major obstacles. There are abundant fertile soils to support an agricultural economy. And the country has both the fossil fuels and other minerals needed to support domestic industrial development. It is unfortunate that political conflicts in the recent past have discouraged tourism and hindered other environment-related aspects of the country's economy.

Archaeological evidence indicates that this ceramic pot found in eastern
Croatia represents a calendar based on the stars.

CHAPTER

3

Croatia
Through Time

C roatia, as is true of all countries in Eastern Europe, has a long
and complex history. This chapter discusses the past and the
people, cultures, and events that have shaped present-day Croatia.

In the Beginning

Archaeological evidence suggests that humans inhabited the area
of what today is Croatia as early as 100,000 years ago. More than a
century ago, a Croatian archaeologist—Dragutin Gorjanovic-Kramberger
—successfully excavated a site near the town of Krapina (located about
30 miles north of Zagreb, near the border with Slovenia). Here, he
found remains of early humans dating back into the Paleolithic
era, or Old Stone Age. It soon became evident that Kramberger had
discovered the world's richest Neanderthal site. The Neanderthal
belonged to a branch of humans believed to have been parallel to

Homo sapiens (all people today). They became extinct some-
time during the period of the last Ice Age. Neanderthal people
lived in groups, were skilled hunters, and many used caves as
shelters and homes. In the decades that followed, Kramberger
discovered many other sites around the country, which was
further confirmation of Croatia having been a major homeland of prehistoric people.

Evidence proves that humans have continuously occupied
Croatia from the Stone Age until now. Under consideration here
are some of the most important early peoples and their culture,
or way of life. One important group was the Starcevo culture.
These Neolithic, or New Stone Age, people were widespread over
almost all of east central Europe—they spanned an area extending from Ukraine on the east, to Bulgaria on the south, and
Croatia on the west. In eastern Croatia, around the city of
Vukovar, archaeologists found household objects dating from the
fifth millennium B.C.E., which was the period of the Starcevo's
culture zenith (highest development). During the next 2,000
years, Vukovar would become the center of the Bronze Age's
Vucedol culture (the name being given from the site near Vukovar,
where most of the associated artifacts were found), which spread
throughout central Europe. Among the more important finds
from this culture is the Vucedolska golubica (Vucedol's dove), a
beautiful piece of pottery now more than 4,500 years old.

Early Historical Era Imprints

Archaeologists and historians differ primarily on the basis
of the evidence they use to interpret the past: archaeologists,
such as Kramberger, use bones and artifacts to interpret history.
Historians, on the other hand, favor the use of historical—or
written—documents. The historical era, then, begins for Croatia
shortly before the beginning of the first millennium B.C.E. The
first mass movement of yet another culture over Croatian
territory can be traced into the Iron Age (1200–700 B.C.E.). This
migration, which is mentioned in the Bible, was an invasion of

a group simply called the Sea People. The movement of Greek and Illyrian tribes from central to south Europe also brought new inhabitants to Croatia. Around 1100 B.C.E., different Illyrian tribes (Illyrians are the ancestors of modern Albanians) colonized parts of Croatia. Most evidence of their existence in Croatia survived in the form of geographical place names. Dalmatia, for example, owes its name to the Illyrian tribe of Dalmats that once lived in the area.

In the first millennium B.C.E., the center of population and culture shifted from the interior region of Croatia to the Adriatic coast. The first Greek colonies appeared on Croatian islands such as Hvar as early as the fifth to fourth centuries B.C.E.. These colonizers brought Greek culture and established towns and trade routes. Soon after the Greeks arrived, Roman influence began expanding toward the eastern shore of the Adriatic Sea. The powerful Romans were able to quickly conquer Croatia and the rest of the Balkan Peninsula. They defeated the last of the Illyrian, Macedonian, Greek, Celtic, and other kingdoms and tribes, thereby establishing Roman domination over Croatia for the next 500 years. Roman rule and culture would bring progress in many forms; it also connected (with the famous Roman road network) these once isolated parts of southeast Europe with other areas of the continent.

The lasting imprint of Roman presence is still evident on the Croatian landscape, especially in the country's architecture. Later chapters will cover Roman cultural influence; however, one important archaeological treasure will be mentioned here—Diocletian's Palace. Emperor Diocletian, who was born in Croatia and ruled over the empire from the late third to early fourth century A.D., built this magnificent structure. The palace is located in what is now downtown Split and is one of the most significant cultural landmarks on the entire Dalmatian coast.

Another major movement of peoples occurred toward the end of the Roman Empire. It was to bring important changes in the ethnic structure of southeastern Europe, including what is now Croatia. Gothic tribes from the east spilled over the borders of the empire, crossing the Danube River in the early fifth century. Asiatic Avars and Indo-European Slavs followed them in the sixth and seventh centuries. Croats were a tribe that belonged to the southern branch of Slavs. They began moving toward the Adriatic coast during the early seventh century. Earliest evidence of a Slavic presence in the area came from information discovered on tombs dated to this period. Slavs penetrated into the Avar Kingdom, which covered a huge area extending from the Dalmatian coast to the steppe grasslands of Eastern Europe. There is little historical evidence of early Slavic existence in Croatia, because there is not much information about the period between the seventh to ninth centuries in Croatia. The single most important bit of historical evidence is found in text written by Byzantium's emperor, Constantine VII Porphyrogenitus, who ruled in the 10th century. Called *De Administrando Imperio* (how to rule an empire), this text basically was written as instructions to his son regarding how the empire should be ruled. Constantine listed the various nations and tribes that lived on the border of the Byzantine Empire. Among those listed are Croatian tribes and their territorial organizations, for which he gave descriptions. It is evident from this document that Slavic peoples already had established numerous settlements on the eastern side of the Adriatic.

Steps Toward Croatian Identity

The first documented existence of Croatian political leaders, historians agree, is dated at the beginning of the 10th century. This written record is traced to an armed conflict between several warlords who called themselves the "dukes." Two of them, Ljudevit, who controlled central parts of Croatia in the area of the Sava River, and Borna, who ruled over coastal areas, went to war against each other. Ljudevit ultimately achieved victory in the conflict.

During the early European Middle Ages (6th–12th century),

most areas controlled by Croatian dukes were located in the coastal area (Dalmatia). Until the 12th century, when Croatia and Hungary created a joint kingdom under the Hungarian ruling house of Arpad, very little evidence existed about Croats' political units in eastern Croatia, the area located between the Sava and Drava Rivers (Slavonia). That is why Croatians today consider their nation's cradle to be the region between the Dinara Alps and the Dalmatian Adriatic Islands.

During the ninth century, a number of dukes—including Vladislav (821–835), Mislav (835–845), Trpimir (845–864), Domagoj (864–876), Zdeslav (876–879), and Branimir (879–892)—ruled semi-independently over their dukedoms. Because of their relatively remote location, they were able to survive the ongoing geopolitical conflict between Byzantium to the east and Charlemagne's Empire of Franks to the west. At that time, another important player appeared on Croatia's shore. Venice, the city-state located on the western, or Italian, coast of the Adriatic Sea, developed into an important trade and military power during the early Middle Ages. The rise of Venice helped to weaken the regional influence of Croatia and its leaders. Antagonism between Croatia and Venice, and among Croatian leaders themselves, continued for several centuries as Venice gained absolute control of the Adriatic Sea.

In the first part of the 10th century Croatian leaders began to establish independent states. This was the time when the most famous Croatian ruler, Tomislav (910–928), expanded his dominance well beyond his own ethnic border. Tomislav, who belonged to the Trpimirovic dynasty (named after the duke Trpimir, 845–864, and his descendants), is an individual who remains controversial in the eyes of historians. Some historians consider Tomislav to have been the first Croatian king, whereas others do not. To modern Croatians, identifying who was the first Croatian king represents one of the most important historical challenges. Tomislav is an important historical person in Croatia because of his possibly having been the country's

King Tomislav is believed by some historians to be the first king of Croatia. He is known for his military achievements and for gaining territory for Croatia during his rule.

first king. He also was an excellent military strategist who successfully defended the country from Hungarians and Bulgarians who were trying to spread their control over the west Balkans. Tomislav's control spread from the coast eastward to the Sava and Drava Rivers on the north and Drina on the east. Under his rule, Croatia achieved its greatest geographical size and military power. For the first time ever, one Croatian ruler had successfully united Dalmatia and Slavonia into one territorial unit.

As often happens, after a strong king dies there is a fight for leadership among his descendants. Following Tomislav's death, there were civil wars that brought much destruction and hardship to Croatia and its people. Some territories were lost. But once the situation was stabilized under a series of new kings the country was able to continue its existence on through the 10th and 11th centuries. By the end of the 11th century, the Croatian kingdom had weakened and external forces were able to make their influence felt in the country's domestic affairs. To make the situation even worse, King Dimitar Zvonimir (1074–1089) did not leave any successors to occupy the Croatian throne. His widow, Jelena, who was related to the Hungarian ruling house of Arpad, decided to support the so-called *Pacta Conventa* with Hungarian King Ladislaus. Some nobles supported Pacta Conventa, but many did not and armed conflict broke out once again. Ultimately, in 1102, after defeat of the opposition, another Hungarian king (Koloman) was successful in gaining control of Croatia, Slavonia, and Dalmatia. This event marked the beginning of the joint Hungary-Croatia state that existed for centuries under different rulers from several dynasties.

Era of Hungarian Control

The heaviest challenge to the Hungary-Croatia state came in 1242 when Mongol forces, under the lead of Batukan, stormed eastern European kingdoms from Asia. Even King Bela IV had to flee Budim, his capital city. He sought help and cover in Croatia—where the Mongols were finally stopped only after news arrived of the death of the supreme Mongolian ruler. Because the people of Zagreb had offered its help to King Bela, he granted the city the status of Free Royal City. This status offered the city a greater degree of autonomy, or independence, in its affairs.

Between the Mongolian invasion in the 13th century and the confrontation with another Asiatic nation in the 16th century, Croatia was relatively calm. Peace was only broken by occasional internal problems and, of course, the seemingly permanent troubles with the powerful Venetians. But the period of relative calm ended when the Ottoman Empire began to expand—including throughout the Balkan Peninsula. Neighboring Bosnia, whose kings were of Croatian origin, was the first to come under attack. It finally surrendered to the Turks in 1463. Belgrade, east of Croatia in what is now Yugoslavia, fell to the Ottoman's in 1521. It was the last obstacle before reaching the plains of eastern Croatia's Pannonian lowlands. The Turks attacked the then combined Hungary-Croatia in 1526. The battle took place on the field next to the Hungarian city of Mohac, with the Turks being victorious. A year later, nobles decided to invite the Habsburgs, the royal family of Austria, to take over rule of Croatia and Hungary. The nobles hoped that by joining the Habsburg Empire, their land would be saved from the Turks. This decision marked the beginning of Croatia's destiny for the next 400 years (until 1918), as part of a joint Austria-Hungary state.

Era of Austria-Hungary Control

To help defend Croatia (and Western Europe), a Military Border region was established in the 16th century in the zone of contact between Europe and the Ottoman Empire. It was organized on the principle of having military garrisons ready for intervention in case of necessity. Land on which to build houses and farms was given to people who were willing to accept military duty. At that time, many of the Serbs living in Turkish controlled areas accepted the invitation and resettled in the Military Border. Until the 18th century, when the power of the Ottoman Empire finally started declining (after the Austrian-Turkish War of 1683–1699), the Military Border would serve as the primary defense. Finally, in 1881, the Military Border was disbanded, and the land was returned to Croatian control. Conflict with the Turks left a lasting imprint on Croatia, one that is evident when looking at the country's borders. It is often said that the country is shaped like a boomerang. Following this description, the inner side (or the alligator's yawning mouth, as described in Chapter 2) follows the old Military Border.

Even though Croatia survived repeated Turkish advances between the 16th and 18th centuries, it was not yet free of outside influences. The country also suffered under the absolute rule of Austrian czars Mary Theresa and Joseph II, as well as a short-lived occupation by forces of French Emperor Napoleon Bonaparte. During the age of absolutism, Austrians tried to officially minimize Croatian independence in its internal affairs. This was a policy they had pursued with other Slavic nations within the Habsburg Empire. One method employed was the Austrian's insistence on the exclusive usage of the German language. This weakened the influence of Slavic-speaking Croatians.

During the 19th century, a wave of nationalistic feelings swept across Europe. In Croatia, growing nationalism contributed to a number of positive changes. For example, in 1847 the Croatian language began to be used exclusively in news publishing, the printing of official documents, and in all aspects of daily life. Earlier, during the 1830s, many intellectuals led by Ljudevit Gaj established the Illyrian Movement. The purpose of the movement was to organize the South Slavs (who, at the time, were incorrectly thought to be descendants of the ancient Illyrians) into one intellectual, cultural, and political body. In the second part of the 19th century, two main factions existed in Croatian political life. People inspired by their identity as South Slavs led the first; they hoped to break free from Habsburgs and form their own Slavic-dominated political unit. People whose political goal was to gain political independence for Croatia formed the second faction. They were not interested in forming a union of Slavic nations. Many Croatians today consider Ante Starcevic, the leader of the second faction, to be the "Father of the Homeland." His was one of the first political voices urging absolute independence.

After the Austrian defeat in their war with Prussia in 1866, some political changes affected Croatia as well. Austria had to reconstruct the Habsburg monarchy and give equal status to Hungary. Two years later, in 1868, a door of opportunity opened for Croatia. It was able to gain limited control over its own internal affairs by signing a similar agreement with Hungary. Even though still within the Habsburg monarchy, for the next several decades, Croatia worked steadily to establish its own national identity in the hope of ultimately establishing its independence.

World War I started in 1914, after the assassination of Francis Ferdinand, the Austrian archduke and successor to the throne, in Sarajevo, Bosnia. Croatia entered the war as a part of the Habsburg monarchy. Four years later the geopolitical (countries and boundaries) picture of Europe was completely different than when the war began. Three major European empires had been destroyed—Russian, German, and Habsburg. With these political changes, Croatia finally got the chance to decide its destiny.

When the war ended in 1918, Slavic nations that were part of the Habsburg monarchy took advantage of the chance for independence. Croatians followed the Czechs, Slovenians, and others in proclaiming their independence. But the road to independence would prove to have many barriers. One problem that quickly appeared was growing Italian imperialism. Italy initially sided with the United States and its Allies (France, England, Russia, and several other countries) against Germany, Turkey, and the Habsburg Empire because it was promised the eastern, Croatian, coast of the Adriatic Sea as its reward.

To stop Italian infiltration in Croatian territory, in the fall of 1918 the Croatian National Council decided to join the new South Slavic union called the Kingdom of Serbs, Croats, and Slovenians. The kingdom was organized on democratic principles and the Serbian king, Petar Karadjordjevic, was selected to rule. Euphoria about the union was short lived, however,

Francis Ferdinand, archduke of Austria, was murdered on June 28, 1914, in Sarajevo, Bosnia. His assassination brought about World War I.

among South Slavs. During the period 1918–1941, strong antagonisms existed between leading Serbian political parties and the main Croatian political power, the Croatian Peasant Party. The events culminated in 1928 when, during the National Assembly meeting in Belgrade, a member of the Serbian Radical Party assassinated the leaders of the Croatian Peasant Party. One of those killed was the party's leader, Stjepan Radic. After this tragic event, the political situation in the Kingdom of Serbs, Croats, and Slovenians deteriorated rapidly. This led King Karadjordjevic to dismiss the Parliament and to proclaim his dictatorship in January 1929. Soon afterward, the country's name was changed to Yugoslavia (which means "country of the South Slavs"). After an agreement between Serbian and Croatian political leaders in 1939, Croatia gained greater autonomy within Yugoslavia.

The newly found autonomy lasted for a short time. In April

1941, Germany invaded Yugoslavia and quickly occupied the entire country. Croatian nationalists who were supported by the German Nazi occupation forces assumed control over Croatia and proclaimed it to be an independent state. This Independent State of Croatia lasted until 1945, the end of World War II. In reality, it was a semi-independent state led by a limited number of pro-Fascists from the Ustase movement and supported by a minority of the Croatian population.

A majority of the population sided with a resistance movement led by forces organized by the Yugoslav Communist Party and its strongman Josip Broz, better known as Tito. Tito's supporters (called Partisans) fought against German-led occupation forces. They also fought against Ustase-organized armed groups that were responsible for concentration camps and the mass executions of Jews, Serbs, Gypsies, and many Croats who were against their rule. After the war, Tito became the leader in Yugoslavia. He formed a Communist dictatorship and strictly controlled and suppressed any nationalistic feelings among Yugoslav nations.

During Tito's rule—which was much more liberal than in other Communist dictatorships—considerable economic progress was achieved. What had been an underdeveloped, primarily agricultural country, became a modern industrialized country. At that time, Croatia became the leading industrial force among the six Yugoslav republics. Although strictly controlled by the Tito government, nationalistic feelings and the desire for independence were still strongly held by some Croatians. In the late 1960s and early 1970s, this nationalist desire became an organized political movement. It even became involved in public protests, resulting in clashes with police that culminated in the arrest of many political leaders. One of those arrested was future Croatian president, Franjo Tudjman, who was sentenced to several years in prison.

Croatia continued to be a part of Yugoslavia until 1991. In 1974 a new Yugoslav constitution gave Croatia more autonomy.

But when the winds of freedom began to blow across Eastern Europe in the late 1980s, it became obvious that most Croatian citizens wanted to live in an independent state. In the first fully democratic elections in over 50 years, Croatian voters elected former dissident and nationalist leader, Franjo Tudjman, to the presidency. Tudjman's Croatian Democratic Union (HDZ) became the leading party in the state's Parliament.

Soon after, a referendum for independence was organized. Most voters supported Croatia's independence from Yugoslavia. The results, however, were sharply divided along ethnic lines. The majority of ethnic Serbs that lived in Croatia wanted to stay in the federation with Serbia and other republics. But the majority of Croatians (who make up almost 80 percent of Croatia's population) decided it was time for independence. These differing views quickly triggered a heated ethnic conflict. By 1995, Croatian forces had finally recaptured Serb-controlled territories and eliminated their pseudo-state called the Republic of Srbska Krajina. The war took approximately 30,000 lives and forced hundreds of thousands of people from their homes. In the West, the conflict was known as the "Serbo–Croatian War." Throughout the rest of this book, it is simply referred to as "the war" or "the conflict." With the end of hostilities, Croatia entered into a period of rebuilding that continues today.

In 1995, President Tudjman was reelected to a second five-year term. But, in 1999, he lost a long battle with cancer. Several months later, in early 2000, separate presidential and parliamentary elections were held. As a result of these elections, a government was formed by a coalition of opposition parties led by the Social Democrats. One of the opposition leaders from the Croatian People's Party, Stjepan Mesic, became the new president; a Social Democrat, Ivica Racan, became prime minister. Today, Croatia is slowly working its way toward achieving political stability and economic prosperity. However, the country faces many of the same problems that beset other East European formerly socialist nations.

Many rural Croatians continue to practice traditional folkways. Autumn is the season of butchering. Smoking pork sausages both preserves meat for the winter months and provides one of the specialties of local cuisine.

4

People and Culture

W ho are the Croats? What are they like? How do they live? What do they do? These are just some of the questions that will be answered in this chapter.

Croatian People

Almost every nation has a legend about its origins, and the Croats are no exception. According to Croat legend, in the distant past several tribes headed by five brothers and two sisters moved into what is today Croatia. The name of one of the brothers was Hrobatos. From his name comes "Hrvat," which translates to "Croat" in Croatian.

It is difficult for modern historians to trace the Croats' past. Little is known about their origin or other aspects of their early history. It is known that the ancient ancestors of present-day Croats left traces of their presence all over central and eastern Europe. If we exclude the explanation drawn from the legend, the origin and meaning of the name Croat remains unknown.

Search for Croat Origins

Scholars have three main theories about Croat origins. The first has to do with early migrations of Slavic people. During the fifth and sixth centuries A.D., Croats broke away and moved from southern Poland and western Ukraine southward toward the Balkan Peninsula. The second theory suggests that Croats originated in Iran and later migrated northward toward the Russian steppes, where they gradually adopted the Slavic culture and later moved on to the Balkans. A third theory considers the Croats not to have been a tribe or nation of peoples; rather, they may have been an order of ancient knights that served as border guards in the Avarian Empire. This belief is supported by the fact that archaeological evidence of Croat presence in central Europe tends to follow the historical border of that ancient empire.

Even if the Croats were not originally members of the larger Slavic nation, they certainly did become assimilated into the Slavic culture. Present-day Slavs are divided into three major groups: eastern, western, and southern. The eastern group includes ethnic Russians, White Russians (Belarus), and Ukrainians; western Slavs are composed of Poles, Czechs, and Slovakians; finally, the southern Slavs include the Slovenians, Croats, Serbs, Montenegrins, Macedonians, and Bulgarians.

As will be discussed later in this chapter, Croatia's ethnic numbers correspond closely to those of the country's religious affiliation. The reason for this seemingly strange relationship is that for more than a century, religion has been used as a primary criterion for ethnic identification. That is, if an individual were Roman Catholic, more than likely he or she—regardless of actual ethnic heritage—would have been identified as being an ethnic Croat. If, on the other hand, the individual were Eastern

Orthodox, then he or she probably would have been classified as being an ethnic Serb. The major ethnic group in Croatia is of course Croats, who make up 78 percent of the total population. Today, Serbs are the second largest ethnic group in the country, accounting for 5 to 6 percent of the population. A variety of other minority groups, including Slovenians, Hungarians, and Muslims, represent small numbers.

Population

The population of Croatia is believed to be about 4.5 million. Estimates range from 4.4 to 4.7 million, but the precise number is unknown. This figure has changed little during the past decade. During the latter part of the 20th century, Croatia's population growth rate was one of the lowest in the world. During the 1990s, however, war took a heavy toll on the country's population and its structure. Between 1991 and 1995, tens of thousands of people were killed. Men, in particular, were lost from the population. Additionally, hundreds of thousands more were displaced from their homes, and many of these people took refuge in other countries.

Life expectancy for Croatians is about 70 years for males and about 78 years for females. Lifestyle, including heavy drinking and smoking, and great stress brought on by the economic uncertainty of recent years, contributes to the much lower figure for males. Even so, these numbers place Croatia on the list of countries with long life expectancy. An aging population can create several problems. As the population grows older, for example, a smaller percentage of a country's people will be in the age group most apt to have children. This, in turn, leads to a declining rate of natural population increase—in the case of Croatia, actually a negative rate. The country's population is declining by approximately 0.2 percent per year. Demographers (scientists who study human populations) believe that by 2050, the country's population may drop to about 3.5 million.

There can be many problems when a population stagnates. These problems include increased health care needs, care for the elderly, and finding enough workers to fill jobs. Today, the population problem is an issue for which the Croatian government is actively searching for a solution.

Way of Life in Croatia

The culture practiced by Croatian people is similar in many respects to that of peoples throughout the region. Language and religion (Roman Catholics, Eastern Orthodox Christians, and Muslims, for example, each differ in some respects) are two major aspects of culture that vary from country to country in southeastern Europe. This section provides details about the way Croatian people live.

Language

Croats are south Slavs and speak a language quite similar to other Slavs. During the early existence of the former Yugoslavia, the Croatian language was officially called Serbo-Croatian, because of the close similarity between the two languages. Since the 1960s, however, Croatian political and linguistic influences have changed the name to Croatian. After the country became independent, great emphasis was given to further development of a pure Croatian language without the influence of the Serbian tongue. National minorities living in Croatia are also allowed to use their own language in most activities, including education and government. The official script is Latin, although use of Cyrillic writing is common among ethnic Serbs living in Croatia.

Some of Croatia's important archaeological evidence, as well as a large segment of Croatia's national heritage, was written in the little-known Glagolitic script. Two monks, Constantine and Method, created this unique script in the ninth century. The monks had been sent by the emperor of Byzantium to Moravia (a region of the Czech Republic) to bring literacy to the local people. Gradually, the script spread to other Slavic groups. The Baska Stone Tablet, dating from the late 11th century, is Croatia's most important Glagolitic object. The tablet was written during the reign of King Zvonimir, who had given some land to the clergy on the island of Krk. Another important work written in Glagolitic is the 13th-century Vinodol Code. It is one of the oldest Slavic legal documents. The code established two legal rights that are accepted throughout most of the world today: the introduction of witnesses into the legal system and protection against the torture of suspects.

Religion

Roman Catholicism is the dominant religion in Croatia. It is practiced by about three out of every four people in the country. Ethnic Serbs and some other minority groups, amounting to some 11 percent of the population, belong to the Eastern Orthodox Church. About 1 percent of Croatians are Muslims, followers of Islam. As is true in a number of countries formerly under Communist rule, a significant number of people consider themselves to be atheists or agnostics.

The Arts and Sciences

During the Middle Ages, the arts flourished throughout the Dalmatian coastal region, particularly in the then independent republic of Dubrovnik (today's city of Dubrovnik and the surrounding area). With its crossroads location between Asia and Europe, Dubrovnik's culture was influenced from both continents. Travelers brought with them products and knowledge never seen before in the West. And Dubrovnik served as a checkpoint on that road. One famous traveler to pass through Dubrovnik was Marco Polo. The Polo family was originally from the Croatian town of Korcula (on the island with the same name), located just north of Dubrovnik. (The name Polo comes from Paulović, which is a variation of

Pavlović.) Eventually, the family moved to Venice, Italy. It was from this trading center that Marco, with his father and uncle, made their famous trip to China during the 13th century. After spending many years with Kublai Khan, the Mongolian emperor, the Polos traveled back to Europe. They had been gone so long that many people had forgotten them.

During the 15th to 17th centuries, literature and science flourished in Dalmatia. Perhaps the most influential writer of the era was Ivan Gundulic. His famous epic, *Osman,* describes the longstanding conflict between the Turks and the Slavic peoples. Another well-known early writer was Marin Drzic. During the mid-16th century, he wrote many popular comedies and works of drama. His best-known work is the comedy, *Dundo Maroje.* Hanibal Lucic and Marko Marulic were authors who produced some of the classic 16th-century Croatian literature. Marulic's epic story *Judita* was about Croats' resistance against the Turks. Today, nearly 500 years after it was written, the book is still widely read by Croatians. During the 16th century, there were also major contributions to science. Marin Getaldic conducted important research in the field of physics and optics. Inventor Faust Vrancic, among other things, contributed to the invention of the parachute.

Croatia's most famous scientist of all time was Dubrovnik resident Rudjer Boskovic, born in 1711. Boskovic spent his career as a professor lecturing at many different universities across the continent. He was highly respected and was honored with memberships in a number of leading European scientific academies. He was an expert in civil engineering and specialized in the construction of astronomical observatories. Boskovic spent nine years in Paris, where he served as the director of naval optics for the French navy.

In the 19th and 20th century, Croatian literature and poetry flourished, with many outstanding works appearing during that time. The Illyrian Movement (a Romantic period) marked the beginning of a sequence of authors that wrote about ordinary

The ancient walled city of Dubrovnik (formerly an independent republic) was a center of culture, learning, and trade during the Middle Ages.

people, including the lower social and economic classes. Among the most important writers are August Senoa, Petar Preradovic, Ante Kovacic, and Silvije Strahimir Kranjcevic.

During the first two decades of the 20th century, Antun Gustav Matos was the leading representative of Croatian literature. Matos also served as the editor of *The Young Croatian Lyric,* an anthology (a collection of works) published in 1914.

During the period between World War I and World War II (1918 and 1940), a series of authors established avant-garde poetry in Croatia. The best known are Tin Ujevic, Dobrisa Cesaric, Dragutin Tadijanovic, and Antun Branko Simic. Miroslav Krleza—perhaps the leading Croatian writer ever— began his work during this period. His "Return of Phillip Latinovic" and "The Glembays" represent some of the best works written during a long, productive, and highly successful career. During World War II, poets Vladimir Nazor and Ivan Goran Kovacic joined the resistance movement during which Kovacic lost his life. After the war, most young writers concentrated their attention on contemporary life in Croatia. It is important to mention that Ivo Andric, who was an ethnic Croat although born at the end of 19th century in Travnik, Bosnia and Herzegovina, received the Nobel Prize for literature in 1961 for his novel *The Bridge on Drina.*

The dawn of the 20th century produced some of the greatest names in Croatian science. Nikola Tesla was born in a poor rural family near the small mountain town of Gospic. He was to become the world's leading engineer. At one point in his career, Tesla worked with American inventor Thomas Edison. His engineering ideas were far in advance of his time. Although he patented hundreds of ideas with the U.S. Patent Office, more than a half-century after his death, scientists still cannot explain some of his patented ideas. When Tesla died, it is most unfortunate that many of his great ideas were lost with him. Some science historians believe that it was Tesla, not Marconi, who invented the radio. Among his other widely recognized contributions are the design of the world's first power machinery—the equipment installed at Niagara Falls. His other major contributions included many inventions relating to the use of electricity, particularly in lighting and telecommunications. Some of his ideas seemed to be rather unrealistic, a fact that brought criticism from some scientists. For example, he believed that communication was possible with other planets; that Earth could be split like an apple; and that he had invented a "death ray" that could destroy planes at a distance of several hundred miles. Nonetheless, today he is regarded as having been one of history's greatest intellects and inventors.

People throughout the world know at least part of the name of a Croatian inventor whose name otherwise is all but unknown—Eduard Slavoljub Penkala. *Penkala* invented the mechanical pen that carries his name. Andrija Mohorovicic, a professor of geophysics at the University of Zagreb, discovered a layer deep beneath Earth's surface that is a key to the study of seismology (earthquakes). In his honor, it is called the Moho layer.

Art also has a long tradition in Croatia. From the Middle Ages, paintings and religious architecture were particularly important. Early churches in the coastal cities of Zadar and Nin stand today as marvels of early (pre-Romanesque, 9th to 10th century) architecture. Also from the same period, archaeologists have found baptismal and other objects with elaborate artistic designs. During the Gothic period (13th to 14th century), beautiful portals were built in cathedrals at Sibenik and Trogir. During the Renaissance (15th–16th century) period and later centuries, Croatian artists continued with productive work in the arts. Julie Klovic and Andrija Medulic produced excellent paintings at that time. In the 19th century, German-born architect Herman Bolle designed many of Croatia's architectural landmarks. Two of the most influential sculptors in the 20th century were Ivan Mestrovic and Antun Augustincic. Both of these sculptors left their mark in the United States as well. Augustincic's statue of a horsewoman can be seen in front of the United Nations building in New York City. Mestrovic's sculptures appear in many American cities, including the widely acclaimed statue of Native Americans in Chicago, Illinois.

Native art is popular in Croatia. Perhaps the best-known school is the one founded by Krsto Hegedusic in the small village of Hlebine. The village produced many important painters, including Ivan Generalic and Ivan Rabuzin, whose works have achieved international acclaim. Croatian films have also achieved widespread recognition. Zagreb's School of Animated Movies is an internationally respected institution with an outstanding reputation. Every year, the International Animated Movies Festival is held in Zagreb. The best-known Croatian animated movie is Dusan Makotic's *The Substitute.* It was the first non-American movie ever to receive a coveted Academy Award.

Spread of Croatians and Their Culture

Croatia is one of the leading European countries—along with Italy and Ireland—in terms of the percentage of its people who have emigrated (left the country). Difficult living conditions pushed many people from their homes toward new countries and a better life. Massive emigration started in the 1880s when phylloxera, plant lice, devastated European vineyards. This destroyed the wine-making industry, leaving tens of thousands of people without employment. The population drain continued through the first quarter of the 20th century. Major destinations included the United States, Canada, Australia, Chile, Argentina, and South Africa. Later in the 20th century—during the 1960s and 1970s— thousands of other Croatians, mainly seeking better jobs, migrated to Germany and other countries of Western Europe. Scholars believe that today there are probably more people with Croatian roots living outside of Croatia than residing in the country itself. Known for their hard work, a majority of emigrants became successful. In the United States, for example, Anthony Maglica (owner of the Maglite Corporation, a manufacturer of flashlights), John Kasich (former Republican Congressman from Ohio), Rudy Tomjanovic (coach of the Huston Rockets professional basketball team), and Dan Marino(vic) (one of the most successful quarterbacks of all time, now retired from the Miami Dolphins) all share Croatia as their ancestral homeland.

What's the Story Behind the Neckties?

Mechanical pens and neckties have one thing in common: both are products that originated in Croatia. Hundreds of millions of people around the world wear ties. Yet few people know why they are wearing a piece of cloth, tightly tied around their neck—other, perhaps, than wanting to "look good." According to history, during the Thirty Years' War in the 17th century, Croatian soldiers used some sort of scarf around their necks. The French soon discovered that scarves not only could be used on the battlefield, but that they also could make a fashion statement. In France, ties replaced traditional collars (which usually were white and therefore easily became dirty). The idea quickly spread throughout France and later to much of the rest of Europe. The French gave the name *Cravate*, which means Croat, to honor the country from which it came. Throughout the centuries, the cravat evolved into various designs. Yet in any form, and now worldwide, the necktie has become the required attire of professional businesspeople.

Contemporary Lifestyle

In many respects, living in Croatia today is much like living in any other European country, sharing similar levels of education, income, and political reality.

Sports and Recreation

Leisure time activities are an important part of Croatia's everyday life. Football (soccer, rather than the American game) and basketball are the most popular and widely enjoyed sports. Other popular sports include handball, tennis, water polo, rowing, and sailing. Croatians have always enjoyed hiking and mountaineering. Many Croatians, including Stipe Bozic, have climbed the world's highest peaks. Some, like alpine skier Janica Kostelic, have won gold medals at the Olympic games. Tennis player Goran Ivanisevic has won the Wimbledon championship. And basketball player Tony Kukoc won several National Basketball Association championships as a member of the Chicago Bulls team. The proudest moment for Croatians since gaining their independence occurred in 1998 when the national soccer team finished third in its first appearance ever in soccer's World Cup competition.

Customs

For most Croatians, life revolves around the family. Family members visit each other often and always bring gifts, especially for children. It is considered impolite to visit somebody's house and not bring gifts. A bottle of spirits or wine for males, coffee or candy for women, and candy for children are the most common types of gifts. Hosts always serve drinks (strong Turkish coffee is always present) and snacks. It is considered impolite to reject this hospitality. When people visit friends or family in other cities, they never stay in hotels; their hosts provide them with a room. In restaurants, a check is never split among friends; one person always pays the bill. The next time, among friends or family, someone else in the group will pay the bill. Kissing on cheeks is common among close friends and relatives when greeting one another. For holidays such as Christmas, people usually travel to see their relatives or join friends for dinner. During their paid vacation, which in

Janica Kostelic is shown here during the women's slalom alpine skiing competition at the 2002 Salt Lake City Winter Olympics. She won the gold medal in the event.

Croatia is usually 3 to 4 weeks per year, many people travel to the coast to enjoy the clear waters of the Adriatic, the national parks, and many other attractions of the region. Many Croatians own a second home or apartment on the coast, where they spend their vacation time. People in Zagreb may also own a holiday home within an easy drive from the city.

There, they spend weekends in relaxation, working on hobbies such as gardening or tending their vineyard. Wine is an important part of Croatian culture.

Cuisine and Diet

Croatian cuisine is basically a reflection of its geography. Away from the coast, Croatian food is similar to that found elsewhere in central Europe. Along the coast, Dalmatian and Istrian cuisine share many similarities with that of Italy. But regardless of where they live, Croatians greatly enjoy food and both respect and appreciate its rich traditions. Breakfast and dinner (evening meal) are lighter than lunch, which normally is the main meal of the day. Black (Turkish) coffee usually is an integral part of the meal; it is served with the main meal, often as an accompaniment to dessert.

The most important factor in the Croatian diet is freshness of ingredients. People in rural areas normally grow their own fruit, vegetables, chickens, and livestock. City residents must use alternative means of obtaining fresh produce and meat. Large urban neighborhoods, particularly in Zagreb, often have an open market called a *Trznica*, where fresh vegetables can be purchased. During winter months, when locally grown fresh vegetables are not available, most people rely on pickled food. Cucumbers, many varieties of peppers, cabbage, cauliflower, mushrooms, and other vegetables are prepared by pickling in the fall and stored in cellars or basements for the winter.

Inland from the coast, the Croatian diet is mostly based on meat, vegetables, and fruits. Pork, beef, and chicken are the major meats consumed; seafood from the Adriatic, or fish caught in local rivers, is served on fewer occasions. Generally, food in the interior is heavier and has more fat content than is common on the coast. Coastal cuisine is typical Mediterranean, most closely related to Italian. Pasta, seafood prepared in various ways, and vegetables are the primary staples. Because of the minimal consumption of red meat and fats, and because olive oil is used in much of the cooking, coastal people rarely experience problems with obesity.

Winemaking dates back to ancient times. It is a process greatly appreciated throughout the county, where both the making and consumption of wine share deep roots in the Croatian culture. In northern Croatia, people traditionally celebrate St. Martin's Day on November 11. This event marks the change of unfermented grape juice into fine wine ready to drink. Currently more than 50 types of grapes are used in wine production. Of domestic wines, the most popular is Dingac. It is made from grapes grown on the Peljesac Peninsula, and it is Croatia's first geographically protected wine (it can indicate the place of origin on the bottle). Dingac is made of Plavac Mali, a grape that is a close cousin to California's popular Zinfandel grape. Oenologists (wine scientists) once believed that the Zinfandel grape was brought to the New World from Italy or Croatia. But it is now recognized that an almost unknown Croatian grape, the Crljenak, is the direct ancestor of the Zinfandel grape. In 1880, Croatian immigrants introduced it into the United States. Croatians' love for wine is most evident in the town of Primosten, hometown of the famed Babic wine. Here, a traveler can see vineyards on the land literally carved out from the rocks in a limestone-dominated landscape.

President Mesic is the head of state and the commander in chief of the armed forces. His five-year term will end in 2005.

5

Government and Economy

S ince 1990, when the one party socialist system was eliminated, Croatia has existed as a parliamentary democracy. A
national constitution was approved in December 1990, and
independence was proclaimed on June 25, 1991. The country's flag
has horizontal bands of red, white, and blue upon which appears
the Croatian coat of arms that includes symbols representing each
of its historical provinces.

Branches of Government

Croatia's government is divided into three branches, the legislative,
executive, and judicial. Each branch has clearly defined responsibilities
and, as is true of the U.S. government, this division represents a
separation of powers.

Legislative Branch

The legislative branch is organized as a unicameral (one branch) Parliament, or National Assembly. Its official name is Hrvatski Sabor. During the 1990s, the Parliament was bicameral with the House of Representatives (Zastupnicki Dom) and the House of Counties (Zupanijski Dom). The latter was abolished in 2000, leaving the House of Representatives as the only legislative body. By law, Parliament cannot have more than 160 members, or fewer than 100. Currently, 151 members of Parliament represent the Croatian voting body. All members are elected by popular secret vote to four-year terms of office. In the 1990s, President Tudjman's Croatian Democratic Union had the majority of seats in the Parliament. During this period, a so-called semipresidential system limited legislative powers, thereby giving more control to the country's president. When opposition parties gained control of the government after the 2000 elections, the system was changed. Now, the Parliament has much more control and the president's powers are more limited. The current president of the Hrvatski Sabor, whose term of office expires in 2004, is Zlatko Tomcic, leader of the Croatian Peasant Party.

Executive Branch

The president of Croatia is Stjepan Mesic. He, like many other Croatian politicians, is a former Communist and a member of the Croatian People's Party. Mesic was elected to a five-year term that will expire in 2005. The president is the chief of state and supreme commander of Croatia's armed forces. His duties include the nomination and appointment of the prime minister. The prime minister also appoints the Council of Ministers, or members of the Cabinet. Finally, the Parliament must approve the appointees. If a majority of representatives in the Parliament do not approve candidacy for a particular candidate, then the prime minister must appoint another candidate and the process is repeated. The current prime minister and the head of the government is Ivica Racan, president of the Social Democratic Party.

Judicial Branch

The judicial branch is made up of the Supreme Court and the Constitutional Court. The House of Representatives elects the Judicial Council of the Republic. This council, in turn, then appoints the judges for both courts. Judges are appointed to eight-year terms. The judicial branch has been criticized for its conservatism—many people believe that it is too slow to modernize. Critics believe that some elements of the former Communist "mentality" still prevail, and they want to see the courts work more effectively.

Armed Forces

Prior to 1991, Croatia was a part of Yugoslavia. It did not have its own military force. When Croatia gained its independence in that year, it also became embroiled in widespread armed conflict. In response to these hostilities, the president created the modern Croatian military structure. As many as 150,000 soldiers served in the armed forces during the conflict of the early 1990s. Today, approximately 30,000 military personnel serve in seven "brigades" each of which includes of about 2,500 soldiers each. Branches of the military include ground forces, naval forces, and air and air defense. The president of the country is the supreme commander of the armed forces.

Foreign Affairs

Croatia's primary foreign affairs goal is to normalize its relationships with its neighbors, including joint work on border disputes. It is also working to become integrated into international organizations such as the European Union (EU). In 1992, Croatia became an official member of the United Nations (UN). Today, its soldiers are serving as peacekeepers in

UN missions worldwide. Its first such assignment was in the African country of Sierra Leone. Croatia is also a member of the Partnership for Peace Program that was organized by the North Atlantic Treaty Organization (NATO). This affiliation is an important first step toward full membership in NATO. In 2000, Croatia took another major step toward international cooperation by being accepted as a member of the World Trade Organization (WTO). Finally, in 2001 the EU and Croatia signed the Stabilization and Association Agreement. This agreement brought Croatia closer to membership in the EU, a goal that the country hopes to achieve during the current decade. At the same time, Croatia is seeking membership in the Central European Free Trade Organization, which would provide another continental economic integration.

Economy

Before 1990, Croatia was the most industrialized of Yugoslavia's former republics. Yugoslavia, itself, ranked among the best-developed Communist governed countries with a centrally planned economy. During this period, Croatia's future seemed bright. At the time, no one expected that the last decade of the 20th century would bring so many changes and such harsh struggles. When armed conflict broke out in 1991, the economy suffered a quick downturn. Today, although peace was restored to the land in the mid-1990s, the economy remains at a pre-1990s level. During the half decade of conflict, trade with its traditional partners in other former Yugoslav republics dropped tremendously. Additionally, significant parts of the communication and transportation networks were under the control of rebel forces. A number of major highways and railroads that were essential to the Croatian economy were under control of Serb forces or within the range of their artillery.

In the period of 1991–1995, Croatia experienced many severe economic problems. These problems included inflation, low wages, and the need to accommodate hundreds of thousands of refugees. The need to pour financial resources into its military further limited the country's potential for economic development. However, the government managed to implement an inflation control program. It was also successful in gradually increasing wages.

Many obstacles to economic development in Croatia are leftovers from the Communist era. One obstacle is the irresponsibility of many high-ranking officials. Often they are not held accountable for past actions. Single party political dominance was interrupted after parliamentary and presidential elections in 2000, when a coalition of opposition parties achieved victory. This event was seen as an important milestone toward economic development and the fight against corruption. The new government seems to be trying to introduce a new approach to economic policy. Yet a low level of achievement and efficiency has left many Croatians unsatisfied. Another major economic hardship results from monopolies controlling some branches of the economy. The oil industry and production of electricity, for example, are each totally controlled by single corporations. A single company also owns the telecommunications network. In the absence of competition, consumers end up paying unreasonably high prices.

Privatization

Croatia, like other former Communist states, is in a sometimes painful economic transition. Under socialist governments, nearly all economic planning was centrally controlled. Now these countries face the challenge of privatizing their economy. If they want to achieve prosperity, they must form a free market (capitalist) economy in which private ownership replaces government control. The market, not the government, also must set prices and wages.

Each country in Eastern Europe has worked on this transition in its own way. And with few exceptions, each of them experienced major problems during this process. In Croatia, critics have accused the former government of having approved poorly written constitutional laws regarding privatization. They also question the government's decision to begin privatization during wartime when legal institutions were unable to monitor and control irregularities. Today most of Croatia's biggest companies are privatized, and the Parliament is working to produce new laws that will encourage economic development. It is also taking necessary steps to ensure Croatia's eventual membership in the European Union.

Energy

As a country's economy grows, so, too, does its consumption of energy. Croatia is not an energy-rich country; it must rely on imports to satisfy its demands for fuel. Domestic oil production is limited to several fields. Oil fields are found in eastern Croatia and in the Adriatic Sea. In the Adriatic, drilling platforms already exist and more are being built and placed into operation. In the northern part of the country, along the border with Hungary, additional petroleum resources have been discovered. During the war years, Croatia was unable to look for oil or to develop oil from the fields in the eastern part of the country. This area was under rebel control until 1995.

Natural gas production, as well as oil yield, is limited. Croatia imports a significant amount of oil to satisfy its increasing domestic demands. In recent years, many towns have been connected to the network of natural gas pipelines. Providing adequate gas for home and industrial use is one of the major projects in the country's attempt to modernize. The government believes that this is the least expensive way to improve the living conditions of its citizens.

The state-owned oil company, Industrija Nafte (INA), holds a monopoly on oil exploration in Croatia. However, in its attempt to expand petroleum production from the Adriatic Sea fields, it has entered into cooperative agreements with foreign companies. One of the areas where exploration is intensive is in the Ivana sector in the northern Adriatic. INA also invests in foreign countries such as Russia, Angola, and Egypt, where it owns some smaller fields.

Perhaps the most important element related to the oil industry is Jadranski Naftovod (JANAF), an oil pipeline. JANAF was built during the era of the former Yugoslavia. It connects the Croatian port of Omisalj on the island of Krk with the country's interior, and extends on to Hungary, Yugoslavia, Slovenia, and Slovakia. The pipeline, which was shut down for years because of war, is in an operative state again. Today, this vital lifeline is becoming increasingly attractive to foreign investors because of its strategic position. JANAF has a capacity of 400,000 barrels per day. If it is connected with the Russian pipeline (Druzba), Russian petroleum from the Caspian area and elsewhere can be exported through the Omisalj port facility. If this plan were realized, it would provide Croatia's economy with a much-needed financial stimulus from pipeline royalties.

Coal and electricity are also essential to economic development and human well-being. Domestic production of coal does not fill the country's needs, and oil must be imported. Croatia does have some reserves of low-grade lignite that are being exploited. Potential for greater production of electricity exists, especially in the form of hydroelectric development. Today, hydroelectric plants generate approximately one-third of all electricity produced in Croatia. Most of these plants are located near the northern city of Varazdin or on the northern coastal region. In the capital and largest city, Zagreb, a substantial portion of its electricity is supplied from three oil-powered plants.

A major setback in Croatian energy development occurred with the 2002 bankruptcy of the American energy company Enron. The company was building a gas-powered electrical plant in Jertovec, which was scheduled to be finished by the end of 2002. Enron was the owner of the power plant and main investor in this project. Therefore, the Croatian government faces a serious problem in filling this void as it works to meet the nation's demand for electricity.

Croatia has finally resolved yet another of its political problems, one pertaining to the former Yugoslavia's only nuclear power plant. The plant, in Krsko, Slovenia, was a joint project between Croatia and Slovenia—but during the time when both were republics of Yugoslavia. When both countries became independent in 1991, the question of ownership was raised. The problem was recently resolved, however, and now Croatia once again receives much-needed electricity from the Krsko nuclear plant. Most of that power is used in Zagreb, which uses nearly a quarter of the country's total energy.

Transportation

Croatia has a transportation network, but needs to expand its mileage of modern expressways. So far only about 570 miles (917 kilometers) of a total 38,070 miles (61,266 kilometers) of paved roads are qualified as highways. The greatest existing need is for a better connection between Zagreb and southern parts of the country, including the coastal cities of Split and Dubrovnik. War delayed construction of these routes for almost a decade. But recently, the American company Bechtel received concessions to build an expressway that will connect the populated north with the remote southern areas of the country. Most local and regional roads also need reconstruction. Of particular importance is the need to improve the main coastal highway. For many years, this was the only route on which tourists could travel along one of the world's most beautiful seashores. Today, however, extremely heavy traffic has far exceeded the highway's capacity, thereby creating a demand for additional routes. As a country that relies heavily on tourism, it is extremely important that Croatia upgrade its highway network.

The railroad network received extensive damage during the war. Although more than one-third of the railroads are electrified, an extensive upgrade is needed. This is particularly true of

Ferryboats, such as this one, shuttle people between the mainland and Croatia's many inhabited islands in the Adriatic Sea.

rail linkages connecting smaller communities. Croatia must also provide transportation links between its various islands, 66 of which are inhabited. Among European countries, only Greece has a more complicated problem of connecting its many islands with its mainland. Hundreds of islands provide beautiful scenery for tourists, but the only way to visit them is by ferry. All inhabited Croatian islands are linked to the mainland by boat, and ferries also connect Croatia with neighboring Italy. Over 20 airports with paved runaways connect major towns. Zagreb's international airport, Pleso, is the home of Croatia Airways, the national air carrier that connects Zagreb with major European cities. There has been a recent emphasis on tourist charter flights. This activity has stimulated construction of smaller airfields that can accommodate charter flights carrying tourists from Western Europe to island destinations in the Adriatic Sea.

Communications

In terms of communications, Croatia is a very "well-connected" country. It has more than 1.5 million telephone lines and a rapidly increasing number of cellular phone users. The main telecommunications company, Croatian Telecommunications (Hrvatske Telekomunikacije), was privatized in 1999. The money received from the sale was used to modernize the network. Today, a modern digital network is being developed to replace the increasingly obsolete analog network currently in use. Cellular phone users can choose among different companies and services. Almost a dozen Internet service providers serve some 150,000 users.

Industrial Production

During the 1990s, industrial production suffered tremendously. As a result, Croatia's unemployment rate is quite high when compared with developed countries. Before the war (1991-1995), most Croatians were employed in the industrial sector. A small number of major companies were able to survive through the troubled times and become serious competitors in the world market. Many smaller businesses, however, still experience problems. Critics place much of the blame on high taxes and a rigid bureaucracy. The country must develop more effective ways to encourage the creation and development of small businesses.

Pliva and Podravka are among the leading Croatian companies and can qualify as multinational corporations. Pliva is one of the main European pharmaceutical companies. Its stocks are being traded on the major international financial

This ship was being built in 1985 in the former Yugoslavia for use by the Soviets. The shipbuilding industry has suffered recently due to Croatia's inability to compete economically in the world market.

markets. The Podravka food company is recognized worldwide for producing high-quality products, including the popular seasoning mix, Vegeta.

Shipbuilding, which has a long history in Croatia, was well developed during the Yugoslav era. But during the past two decades, it has experienced a decline, resulting from an inability to compete with cheaper builders in South Korea and elsewhere. Recently, however, foreign buyers have once again recognized the quality of Croatian shipbuilding and the number of orders is steadily increasing.

Agriculture

Agriculture in Croatia has tremendous potential. The country's physical environment makes it possible to grow a great number of different crops. Adequate moisture and relatively warm temperatures also help to ensure high yields. Dairy and meat production, centered mainly in interior Croatia, has been practiced for a long time. But it is still not developed to the level of Western standards. In the Mediterranean climate region of the Dalmatian Coast and on the Adriatic islands, excellent olive oil and some splendid wines are produced. Although little known beyond the country itself, Croatian wine is among the world's best. Excellent Chardonnays and Rieslings come from the interior. Other grapes, mainly local or Italian, thrive in the seaside environment. Farmers are eager to achieve higher levels of production, sales, and income. But they face many obstacles that ultimately lead to lower production, stagnant sales, and relatively low revenue for their efforts. Low government subsidies and high taxes combine to limit income. Imported foods are often less expensive than those domestically grown. Also, there is very little international advertising of Croatian food products and wines. Therefore, there is little demand in foreign markets.

Trade

In terms of balance of trade, Croatia imports nearly twice as much as it exports. This creates a huge deficit of more than three billion dollars each year. The major export commodities are food, textiles, and chemicals. Imports include electronic equipment, vehicles, food, machinery, oil, and lubricants. Germany is Croatia's main trade partner; it is responsible for almost 16 percent of exports and about 18 percent of imports. Other important trade partners are Italy, Slovenia, Russia, Austria, and Bosnia and Herzegovina. The United States imports some $85 million per year—primarily food and textiles. The United States also exports an average $250 million in goods to Croatia each year.

Tourism

Currently, tourism is the most profitable economic activity in Croatia. In 2001 it generated nearly $3.7 billion in national income. The country has excellent potential to become a primary world tourist destination during both the summer and winter months. The climate is pleasant year-round. Many tourist destinations enjoy some of Europe's highest number of hours with sunny skies. With the dry summers characteristic of the Mediterranean climate, weeks may pass without rain. But in the winter, as well, the sky remains quite cloud-free much of the time.

Unfortunately, Croatia is still suffering from the turbulence of the 1990s and has yet to return to a pre-1990 level of tourism. There are fewer tourist resorts in the country today than there were during the pre-1991 socialist era. In 2000 the total number of tourist visits (including Croatians visiting tourist sites and facilities) was 6.5 million. This figure represents about two million fewer tourists than visited a decade earlier. Most of the foreign tourists come from Germany, the Czech Republic, Poland, and Austria.

Nautical tourism (people arriving by boat, often their own) has developed rapidly. By the year 2002, nearly 50 marinas were available for tourist use. Additionally, tourism based on hunting wild game, such as deer and pheasant, has increased greatly during recent years. With around 770 hunting districts, Croatia offers ample opportunity to hunt both big and small game. The country also attracts tourists to health resorts and spas, which are based on mineral springs. Again, this type of tourism also declined sharply during the 1990s. With a rebuilding of the infrastructure, it should once again attract tourists.

The province of Zagorje has experienced economic and population growth in recent years. The region has farms as well as castles, and its mineral springs attract tourists to local spas.

CHAPTER

6

Regions and Cities

Geographers often divide the world and its various areas into regions. A region is an area that is united in some way by one or more elements. In the United States, for example, people often speak of the "South," or the "Midwest." Croatia is divided into several regions. Chapter 2 discussed Croatia's three basic land regions and two regions defined by climatic differences. Croatia, by world standards, is a rather small country, yet it can be divided into several distinct regions. This chapter presents five regions—each of which has its own unique characteristics. They are central Croatia (Zagreb and its surroundings); eastern Croatia (including Slavonia, Baranja, and Srijem); the mountains (Gorski Kotar and Lika); the north Adriatic (Hrvatsko Primorje and Istra); and the south Adriatic (Dalmatia). Each region has at least one dominant city. Since the 1990s, the country has been divided politically into 20 counties. But these political regions do not always coincide with the geographic regions discussed below.

Central Croatia

Central Croatia is the country's geographic heart. It is the most densely populated region of the country and also is the nation's economic, political, and cultural center. This core region is sandwiched between Slovenia to the west, Hungary to the north, and Bosnia and Herzegovina to the south. It is home to several important urban centers, including the country's capital and largest city, Zagreb, and smaller regional provincial cities, including Varazdin, Karlovac, and Sisak. The physical landscape is a combination of mountains and river valleys. Each of these cities is located on a major river, yet Sisak is the only city that can be linked by water to other locations in Europe. River barges and boats can travel on the Sava River, which is navigable to Sisak, into the Danube. And from the Danube, much of Europe is accessible by a tight network of rivers, canals, and seas.

Zagreb

Zagreb grew from a position on the foothills of Medvednica Mountain overlooking the Sava River Valley. The area now occupied by Zagreb actually was settled during the Roman Empire. The town of Andauntonia existed during the early centuries of the Christian era on the banks of the Sava River at a site now located within Zagreb's city limits. Zagreb, itself, was first mentioned in the late 11th century. At that time it was just a small town known for its Catholic dioceses. At the dawn of the 12th century, the area in which Zagreb is located changed political hands, with control shifting from Croatia to Hungary. With the transition, Zagreb's geographical location helped it become an important crossroads, rather than an isolated cultural backwater. Through the centuries the city expanded greatly in size and importance. Ultimately, it became the capital of the ethnic Croat people. Since the mid-19th century, Zagreb has experienced rapid population growth, exploding from 10,000 people in 1850 to nearly 1 million in 2002.

In the former Yugoslavia, Zagreb was the country's primary industrial and cultural center. Even though the city suffered greatly during the decade of the 1990s, it is still one of the leading East European urban centers. It is an important transportation crossroad between western and southeast Europe and Asia Minor. After the fall of Communism in Eastern Europe, countries could participate in free trade with any country. This greatly increased Zagreb's importance because of its ports on the Adriatic Sea and because it is located on the main highway and railroad between the landlocked countries of Hungary, Slovakia, and the Czech Republic. The city is an important business and manufacturing center and home to some of Croatia's biggest companies.

Zagreb has long been the country's most important educational center. The University of Zagreb, established in 1669, is one of the oldest institutions of higher education in southeastern Europe (Harvard University, the oldest in the United States, was established in 1636). Throughout its history, numerous scientists studied and worked in Zagreb. Some of them, such as Lavoslav Ruzicka and Vladimir Prelog, became Nobel Prize laureates. The university began as the Jesuit Academy of the Royal Free City of Zagreb, but in 1669 the Habsburg emperor signed a document that upgraded the academy to university status. The University of Zagreb's modern history began in 1874 when the Croatian Parliament produced a document that finally changed the name from academy to university. Today, the University of Zagreb has over 40,000 students. The Ministry of Science has been trying in recent decades to decentralize higher education and to establish branches of the university in smaller towns such as Varazdin.

Zagreb has many attractions and is developing as a tourist destination. The city is divided into three major sections—

ancient Upper Town, the century-old Lower Town, and the more recently settled areas. Upper Town is the original town site, or historical core. It is located on two hills overlooking the Sava River. During the Middle Ages, two hills were settled, each with its own particular groups of inhabitants. First, Kaptol (one of the hills) was a residence of the Roman Catholic bishop and other Catholic clergy. The opposite hill, called Gradec, was reserved for everybody else. The bridge that connected the two parts of town was called the Blood Bridge. The name is a legacy of the often-bloody conflicts that took place between the early Catholic clergy and other residents of the city. The Gothic style Cathedral of St. Stephen was built during the Middle Ages. But it got its present monumental character when it was restored in neo-Gothic style in the 19th century. Today it represents not only an important landmark in the city of Zagreb, but it is also one of the world's tallest buildings made of rock. Herman Bolle, the German architect who restored the cathedral, also designed the monumental arches at Zagreb's main cemetery, Mirogoj, another historical landmark. The old observatory and Museum of the City of Zagreb are located on the neighboring hill that was home for ordinary citizens.

Lower Town is noted for its distinctive Secessionist (art nouveau) architectural style. Many of its buildings are of this unique architectural design that was popular within the Habsburg monarchy during the late 19th and early 20th centuries. A number of museums and art galleries were built during this period. So were the buildings of the Croatian Academy of Arts and Science and the Croatian National Theater. These structures are located in the so-called green horseshoe, a complex of parks built in the same period. The Ante Topic Mimara Museum, located nearby, is one of the most popular in Zagreb, and resembles London's famed Buckingham Palace in design.

Zagreb is proud of its many parks and recreational sites. In fact, so much space within the city is wooded that it is one of Europe's greenest cities. The largest and most popular park is

Maksimir. It is located several miles east of the town center. Woodlands, lakes, trails, an adjacent zoo, and other amenities attract thousands of visitors on pleasant weekends and throughout the year. Citizens also enjoy hiking in the hills of Mt. Medvednica. It was on this 3,380-foot high (1,030 meters) and nearly 20-mile long (32 kilometers) mountain that Zagreb was built. Today, the mountain offers a striking panoramic view of the city and surrounding valleys below. Hiking and mountaineering are popular in Croatia. There are many clubs devoted to these activities; people plan trips, join together in outdoor ventures, and share experiences with others. Medvednica's highest peak is Sljeme. On clear days from atop this peak it is possible to see the Austrian Alps, located almost 100 miles away. In the winter, many residents of Zagreb are drawn to Sljeme's slopes, several of which have trails and ski lifts. Croatia Television's transmission tower rises above the peak. During the military conflict of the 1990s, the tower was heavily damaged due to a direct hit from a missile, but it was later repaired.

Across the Sava River is New Zagreb. This is a modern area, built mainly during the past 40 years. It is popularly called "the bedroom," because most of its residents work or study in the city during the day and go home to their apartments in New Zagreb in the evening. During the 1960s, industrialization was developing rapidly in Croatia. Zagreb needed to provide additional living space for thousands of workers who were moving to the city. New Zagreb was built under the then Socialist controlled urban planning system. Today more than 100,000 people live in New Zagreb.

One of the seemingly never-ending problems in Croatia's capital is the city's outdated infrastructure—the various networks, including streets, bus lines, water mains, sewage and gas pipelines, electricity, communications, and other things that allow a city to function. Old cities may offer wonderful history, scenery, and culture to the tourist, but they can be very difficult to keep functioning. In Zagreb, the sewage system and gas pipelines must be improved in older neighborhoods; many roads need to be rebuilt, or repaired; and tram and bus lines must be expanded. If Zagreb is able to update its infrastructure, it will be one of Europe's most impressive cities.

Several smaller communities around Zagreb belong to a group of so-called satellite towns. These towns include Samobor, Zapresic, and Velika Gorica. People live here and commute to Zagreb on a daily basis, most using the public transportation system. Vrbovec, 20 miles east from Zagreb, is a meatpacking center. PIK, a company from Vrbovec, is one of the major food suppliers in Croatia.

Touring the Region

The economy of central Croatia is based on a combination of agricultural and industrial production. For many people who live in villages near urban areas, farming represents an additional source of income. The province of Hrvatsko Zagorje is between Zagreb and Varazdin. Until recently, it was a beautiful, though economically little developed, region that supported only a small and scattered population. During recent decades, however, its economy has shown marked development and the population has experienced sharp growth. Small family-owned businesses with a few employees are the core of that development. This has helped to stabilize migration out of smaller rural communities toward Zagreb and Varazdin. Zagorje also has the potential to become an important tourist destination. Mineral springs in Krapina, Tuhelj, Donja Stubica, and Varazdin have been used as spas for a long time. Every year, thousands of people enjoy the health benefits afforded by the spas located in these cities.

The region also has a rich history. Zagorje may have more hilltop castles than any other area of comparable size in the world. For centuries, beginning in medieval times and continuing well into the 19th century, nobles built castles, towers,

The northern city of Varazdin on the Drava River was once the capital of Croatia. Today the city has a combination of attractions, including mineral springs and entertainment, notably its "Baroque Evenings."

and towns. Today, these intriguing bits of history reflected in stone and timber are scattered about the region's landscape for tourists to see and enjoy. Some of them are restored as museums; others, such as the Bezanec Castle, have been converted into modern hotels.

Varazdin is a town on the Drava River that at one time was the Croatian capital. Today, it is the main city in far northern Croatia, the area near the border with Slovenia. Home to some

50,000 people, present-day Varazdin combines old charm and modern style. Baroque architecture and a large medieval castle (old town) dominate the center of the city. The city often hosts events such as culturally inspired "Baroque Evenings." Varazdin's economy is based on several large manufacturing companies and numerous smaller businesses. Its most important industry is Varteks, which, among other textile products, makes Levi's jeans. The beverage producer Vindija is the second largest company in Varazdin. It is among the leading Croatian beverage producers and employs hundreds of people.

The old historical crossroad, Sisak, is best known as the location of Croatia's victory against the Turks in 1593. Today it is a center of oil refining and steel production. The city, located at the juncture of the Sava and Kupa Rivers, has a population of some 60,000 and has become an important regional center. The meat company Gavrilovic is headquartered in the neighboring town of Petrinja. It is one of Croatia's largest and most popular food producers, with many of its products being made for foreign markets.

When passing between northern and southern Croatia on the country's major highway, travelers must go through the city of Karlovac. The strategic importance of this location—on Croatia's five rivers and at a point where the country narrows between its northeastern and southwestern regions—was recognized long ago. In the 16th century, the Habsburg Archduke Karl decided to build a military fortification there. The role of this fortified castle, built in the shape of a six-point star, was to prevent intrusion and attacks by Turks from neighboring Bosnia. The importance of the castle to people then living in this part of Croatia is indicated by the fact that the city's name, Karlovac, celebrates its founder. With around 70,000 inhabitants, Karlovac is the second largest city in central Croatia. During the war, some of Karlovac's suburbs experienced heavy damage. Rebuilding of these suburbs began in the mid-1990s and continues today.

Eastern Croatia

Eastern Croatia includes the provinces of Slavonia, Baranja, and Srijem. It is a large area that occupies approximately one-third of the country's total land area. Agriculture is the primary economic activity in the region. Western portions of Slavonia are mostly hilly to mountainous. The six dominant upland areas are Papuk, Psunj, Krndija, Pozeska Gora, Dilj, and Bilogora. In its eastern part, between the mountains and the Danube River, the land is quite flat. Here, fields of corn, wheat, sunflowers, and sugar beets dominate the landscape.

The economic, administrative, educational, and cultural center of eastern Croatia is Osijek, a town of 130,000. Modern Osijek was built near the remains of Mursa, a town established during the Roman period. Osijek, which is still developing into a modern European city, has some impressive architecture. The Church of St. Peter and Paul dominates the town's skyline with its 300-foot (91 meters) spire. Most of the landmark buildings date to the turn of the 19th and 20th centuries; yet, some Baroque architecture can be seen in old parts of town. The most important company is Belje, an agricultural giant (by local standards). It has processed local agricultural products for centuries and is the best example of the region's economic orientation.

Smaller, yet important, regional centers include Vinkovci, Vukovar, Slavonska Pozega, Virovitica, Koprivnica, and bordering Bosnia on the Sava River, Slavonski Brod. The food processing company Podravka is recognized as one of the first Croatian multinational corporations. The company employs thousands of people from Koprivnica and the surrounding towns. Its most famous product is Vegeta, a mix of more than a dozen vegetables that is considered to be an essential component of central European cuisine. Before the war, Vukovar, a town on the banks of the Danube, was one of the wealthiest and most beautiful places in Croatia. Sadly, armed conflict in 1991 led to the complete destruction of Vukovar. Hardly any buildings survived without major damage. Once a prosperous town, it is now undergoing a long and costly rebuilding process.

Mountains (Lika and Gorski Kotar)

A region of extensive mountains serves as a barrier between Croatia's inland northeast and its Adriatic coastal area. This rugged, remote, and sparsely populated area is the country's least developed. With its breathtaking natural beauty, the mountain region has tremendous potential for tourism. But this development will not occur in the foreseeable future. The area was ravaged by the conflict of the 1990s. And today more people are leaving the mountains than are moving into the region, and its economy is in decline. The government believes that its meager resources must be spent in developing other parts of the country.

One of the region's primary attractions is the Plitvicka Jezera (Plitvice Lakes) National Park. It attracts tourists who come to see its 16 lakes and dozens of spectacular waterfalls. Many Westerners used to come to the park to celebrate weddings at the base of the waterfalls, but this popular practice was discontinued during the war years of the early 1990s. With the political situation now somewhat stabilized, tourists are once again returning. The park is also on the UNESCO World Heritage List.

The Bjelolasica mountain resort is the main Croatian winter sport center. Risnjak National Park, located between Delnice and Rijeka, is a popular hiking destination, and the only area in Croatia with elements of alpine authenticity. The traveler can experience one of the most beautiful sunrises in Croatia by standing atop Mt. Risnjak. Many other places of interests are connected with Premuziceva Staza (Premuzic's Path), a highway for hikers that winds throughout Gorski Kotar for more than 30 miles. Major towns in Croatia's mountain region are Gospic, Ogulin, Otocac, and Delnice. Industrial production is limited and employment opportunities are few, factors that contribute to a drain of young people who are drawn by opportunities in larger cities.

North Adriatic

Croatia's Adriatic coastal region differs greatly from the country's interior. In many respects, the entire coastal area is quite similar. Yet Croatians think in terms of two coastal regions—the North Adriatic and the South Adriatic, or Dalmatian Coastal Region. The North Adriatic focuses upon the dominant city of Rijeka. It is an old city whose history dates back to the Roman times. Today, Rijeka is the country's third largest city. It is Croatia's main port. Major industries in the area surrounding Rijeka include shipbuilding and oil refining. The nearby city of Opatija is one of the oldest tourist centers in the country. Tourism here began during the second half of the 19th century, primarily as a resort for the Austrian upper socioeconomic class. Today, it is still a top-notch resort that attracts many West Europeans to the Adriatic shores.

Well-preserved ruins from the Roman age—such as a large amphitheater, a triumphal arch, and the temple of Augustus and Roma, all from the first century A.D.—are in the city of Pula at the southern edge of the Istrian peninsula. Pula is the largest city in Istrian county. From its beginning nearly 2,000 years ago, it has always benefited from its strategic location. Modern Pula is an important industrial and tourist center. The main economic activity on the Istrian Peninsula is tourism. Because of its proximity to Italy, Austria, and Germany, no county in Croatia receives more foreign tourists than does Istria.

Brijuni National Park occupies several islands located a few miles off the southwest coast of the Istra Peninsula. These islands have been inhabited since Neolithic times. One might imagine that these early settlers were attracted to the islands thousands of years ago because of the pleasant climate, strategic location, and scenic beauty. Later, during the first century A.D., Romans settled in the region, perhaps for the same reasons. About a half-century ago, the late President Tito of the former Yugoslavia recognized the same qualities and, as a result, chose to build his summer residence there. As recently as the 1990s, the late Croatian President Tudjman made the same decision, enjoying his summers on Brijuni. Several years ago paleontologists discovered dinosaur foot prints on Brijuni's seafloor. It seems that even Jurassic creatures enjoyed the island's beauty.

South Adriatic (Dalmatia)

Dalmatia perhaps is best known to many Americans as having been the home of the popular breed of dog seen in the film, *101 Dalmatians*. Travelers to the region are rewarded by its spectacular natural beauty and rich cultural heritage. After Slavic peoples migrated from central to southeast Europe during the seventh and eighth centuries, Croats permanently settled in Dalmatia. The region became the cradle of their nation. Today it is a major tourist destination. It offers some of the world's most spectacular examples of karst topography (landform features) and some of the clearest seawater in the world—all backed by a range of mountains. The region's splendid architecture and many monuments are a legacy of the South Adriatic's rich cultural heritage, some of which dates back to the Roman Empire and the beginning of Christianity. Split, the biggest town and the unofficial regional "capital," serves as an excellent example of Dalmatia's fascinating physical, cultural, and historical geography.

Split

When Roman Emperor Diocletian, who ruled at the end of the third and beginning of the fourth century, grew tired of tormenting Christians, he liked to relax in his palace. That

The busy port city of Split developed around the Diocletian's Palace. Today, Split is the second largest, as well as one of the oldest, cities in Croatia.

magnificent structure was built on the shore of the Adriatic Sea not far from the town of Salona. Later, when Avars attacked, Salonians took refuge in the palace and started building a settlement from which grew modern Split, a town of 200,000 people.

Diocletian's palace today occupies a large area of downtown Split. The famous site is included on the UNESCO World Heritage List. The city's cathedral, once part of the emperor's mausoleum, belongs to the group of oldest Christian churches in the world. The Cathedral offers evidence of nearly 2,000 years of history, and it is the pride of the city of Split. Riva, a walkway near the sea, and Marijan Park are places where the citizens of Split can enjoy walking, recreation, and the easy-living Mediterranean lifestyle. Because of its geographic location and dominance over Dalmatia, Split is one of the fastest growing cities in Croatia and today ranks as the country's second largest. The local university attracts students from all over Dalmatia and the rest of the country as well. Split also has several museums and an excellent oceanographic institute.

The southern Croatian city of Dubrovnik is known as the "Jewel of the Adriatics." Because of its beauty, and cultural and historical importance, the entire old town part of the city is listed as one of UNESCO's World Heritage Sites. For centuries, Dubrovnik was an independent republic, a status it retained until 1797 when it was conquered by Napoleon's forces. Later, it became part of the Habsburg Empire and Croatia. During its period of independence, Dubrovnik played an important role as a major center of trade between Asia and Europe. Well-preserved fortresses and city walls rise above the old town. Beautiful 14th-century Franciscan and Dominican monasteries were totally destroyed by a devastating earthquake in 1667, but they were later rebuilt. Inside the Franciscan monastery is the famous Dubrovnik pharmacy, built in 1317. This is the third oldest pharmacy in Europe and is the oldest still open. The city also has the third oldest synagogue in Europe. During the war some of Dubrovnik's monuments were heavily damaged. But the government has helped to repair damage and to return some of the old shine to this beautiful city. Today, Dubrovnik once again is a regular port of call for most Mediterranean cruise ships.

Zadar and Sibenik are another two important towns in Dalmatia. Both of them have many monuments. The best known are the church of St. Donat, built in the 9th century in

Zadar, and the 15th-century St. James cathedral in Sibenik. The later represents a unique blend of Gothic and Renaissance architectural styles. Not far from Sibenik is Krka National Park. Breathtaking waterfalls created by water cascading over limestone deposits make Krka a wonderful destination. A short boat ride from Sibenik is Kornati National Park. The park is a group of almost uninhabited islands that offer outstanding scenery.

New Years is a traditional time for people around the world to take stock of where they are and express their hopes for the future. After many years of conflict and economic hardship, Croatians look forward to more normal, safe, and prosperous times.

7

Future of Croatia

Although its recent past has been quite troubled, Croatians are optimistic about their country's future. But it is up to them to ensure that the future is, indeed, bright. The country shares many of the same problems that hinder stability and development in most other former Eastern European socialistic states. Achieving political and economic stabilization is an essential first step to reaching Western levels of living. A stifling bureaucracy remains a strong legacy of Communism, and it serves as a strong barrier to internal development and foreign investment in Croatia's future. For a country such as Croatia, foreign investments are essential if its economic condition, including the prosperity of its people, is to improve.

For decades, tourism has been the primary contributor to Croatia's economy. Additionally, it was the major source of fresh capital for the government's annual budget. During the war years of the first half of the 1990s, tourism declined to almost nothing. This factor, together with vast defense expenses, caused a tremendous drop in the country's economy. Since recovery always occurs more slowly than destruction, it will take much more than five years for Croatia to return to pre-1990 economic levels. And a much longer period of time—perhaps decades—will be needed to catch up to the levels of development currently enjoyed in Western Europe and the United States.

Major investments must be made in redeveloping the tourist industry, which has been the foundation of Croatia's economy. The country hopes to develop as an "elite" tourist destination. This, of course, is a logical goal expressed by nearly all countries that rely on tourism as the major source of income. One of the best examples of that policy is Spain, a country that shares some similarity with Croatia. Spain, however, has invested much more capital in the development of its tourist potential than has Croatia—and the results are obvious. Spain's Costa del Sol is one of the world's most popular tourist destinations. Croatia, on the other hand, has but one major two-lane highway that passes through its coastal area, thereby making travel and access by land quite slow and difficult. In Chapter 2, it was mentioned that the bora (a strong wind common to the coastal region) can close the coastal highway for hours and sometimes days. When this happens, traffic either stops, or drivers take inland routes, away from the coast and its tourist facilities. During the peak tourist season of June through August, the traffic on coastal roads in Dalmatia is so heavy that it almost comes to a standstill. After the war, the government's priority was to start building a four-lane expressway that would connect Zagreb and Dalmatia. When this project is realized it will remove most of the heavy trucks from the coastal roads, lower the number of accidents, and make traveling more enjoyable to tourists.

Wine production, as previously mentioned, has enormous potential in Croatia. There are hundreds of varieties of domestic

Croatia's wine industry has received some international attention. In the United States, Representatives on Capitol Hill participated in a wine-tasting event.

grapes, many of which have been imported and cultivated with great success. In recent years, Croatian wines have been recognized for their high quality, receiving gold medals in international wine competitions. Unfortunately, however, heavy-handed bureaucracy, complicated laws, and high taxes levied on the industry do not allow the improvements that are necessary if Croatian vintners are going to keep up with world-wide competition. Croatia must do more to promote its wines. Once they become recognized for their quality, vineyards and wineries will become yet another tourist attraction. Wine tourism is becoming increasingly popular in the world today, drawing travelers to France, Italy, California's Napa and Sonoma Valleys, Australia, and other famous areas of production. Interest in wine consumption has increased during recent years; this is particularly true since medical researchers have established that the moderate drinking of red wine by adults can help fight against heart disease. Many countries create and promote so-called wine routes as primary tourist attractions, and Croatia definitely can be one of them.

Many Croatians see their future closely tied to that of the European Union (EU). Achieving this goal is perhaps the government's top priority. Membership in the EU would be a major step in elevating Croatia to the economic and political level comparable to that of today's Western European states. Also, before the war Croatia had extensive economic relations with other republics of the former Yugoslavia. Since 1991, however, many of these connections have been severed. Croatia must work to improve its relations with neighboring countries. Ideally, within the next few years they will return to, if not surpass, the pre-1991 level of cooperation.

Displaced people are another major problem that stems from the war of the early 1990s, including thousands who remain in Croatia (and Croatians elsewhere). Tens of thousands of people fled their homes because of the fighting and became political refugees in neighboring countries. Today, the former republics are cooperating with one another on this serious problem. But it will take years before all people can be returned to their homeland. For many of them, of course, their homes and villages were completely destroyed—so they have no home to which to return.

Yet another significant problem faced by Croatia and neighboring Bosnia and Herzegovina is that huge areas are still covered with land mines. Hundreds of thousands of mines, most of them designed to destroy human extremities and render the victim handicapped, were scattered about the land. Before the war, much of the land was used for agriculture. As life has returned to normal, the land mines continue to pose a constant danger to farmers working their fields, children playing in the country, and young and old alike venturing into the rural landscape. Removal of the mines is a slow, dangerous, and expensive process that will take years to complete. Even though the UN sponsors a land mine removal program offering financial and technological support, people continue to die from land mine explosions in the countryside.

Croatia has one major advantage that should be of primary importance in terms of the country's future—that is its people. American scientist Theodore Schultz, a 1979 Nobel laureate in economics, said that each country's most important capital asset is its own people. Most of Croatia's people are very well educated and have attained rather high cultural norms. An accent on education is every family's main goal. The country's educational institutions no doubt produce more scientists and skilled professionals than the country's current economic capacity can absorb. Unfortunately, during the harsh conditions of the last decade many young people emigrated from Croatia in search of a better life. As is true in countries throughout the world, the 21st century will belong to the generations of young, well-educated, dedicated, hardworking citizens who will become their country's most important capital. In this respect, if Croatia can achieve a level of stability and development that will help retain the young people in its population, the country will be truly blessed and its future will be bright.

Country Name	Conventional—Croatia
	Local—Hrvatska
Location	Southeastern Europe, between the Adriatic Sea and Danube River
Capital	Zagreb
Area	21,829 square miles (56,538 square kilometers)
Land Boundaries	Total: 1,260 square miles (2,028 kilometers)
Border Countries	Bosnia and Herzegovina, 579 miles (932 kilometers); Hungary, 204 miles (329 kilometers), Yugoslavia, 165 miles (266 kilometers); Slovenia, 311 miles (501 kilometers)
Climate	Continental climate in the north and east, Mediterranean on the Adriatic coast, mountain in the central region
Highest Point	Dinera (1,830 meters)
Land Use	Arable land: 21 percent
	permanent crops: 2 percent
	permanent pastures: 20 percent
	forests and woodland: 38 percent
	other: 19 percent (1993 est.)
Natural Hazards	Floods, forest fires, earthquakes
Environmental Issues	Acid rain and pollution from industry, forest fires in coastal region during summertime, land mine removal
Population	4,381,352 (2001 est.)
Population Growth Rate	1.48 percent (2001 est.)
Life Expectancy at Birth	Male, 70.38; Female, 77.7; Total Population, 74
Ethnic Groups	Croat, 78.1 percent; Serb, 12.2 percent; Muslim, 0.9 percent; Hungarian, 0.5 percent; Slovenian, 0.5 percent; Others, 8.1 percent
Religions	Roman Catholic, 76.5 percent; Eastern Orthodox, 11.1 percent; Muslim, 1.2 percent; Others, 11.2 percent
Languages	Croatian—official; other languages used in limited circumstances
Literacy	98 percent

Type of Government	Presidential/parliamentary democracy
Head of State	President
Independence	June 25, 1991 (from Yugoslavia)
Administrative Divisions	20 counties, 1 city (Zagreb)
Flag Description	Red, white, and blue horizontal bands with Croatian coat of arms (red and white checkered)
Currency	Kuna (HRK)
Real GDP growth	4.3 percent (2001 est.)
GDP–Per Capita	Purchasing power parity–$5,800
Inflation Rate	4.8 percent
Natural Resources	Oil, bauxite, low-grade iron ore, calcium, natural asphalt, mica, clays, salt, and hydropower
Industries	Chemicals and plastics, machine tools, fabricated metal, electronics, pig iron and rolled steel products, aluminum, paper, wood products, construction materials, textiles, shipbuilding, petroleum and petroleum refining, food and beverages; tourism
Exports	$4.3 billion (f.o.b., 1999)
Export Partners	Italy, 18 percent; Germany, 15.7 percent; Bosnia and Herzegovina, 12.8 percent; Slovenia, 10.6 percent; Austria, 6.2 percent (1999)
Imports	$7.8 billion (1999)
Import Partners	Germany, 18.5 percent; Italy, 15.9 percent; Russia, 8.6 percent; Slovenia, 7.9 percent; Austria, 7.1 percent (1999)
Transportation	Highways, total: 17,300 miles (27,840 kilometers)
	Railways, total: 1,427 miles (2,296 kilometers)
	Waterways: 488 miles (785 kilometers)
	Airports: 67

100,000 B.C.E.	Evidence of early humans in Croatia.
2500 B.C.E.	Zenith of Vucedol culture.
1100 B.C.E.	Illyrian tribes settle in Croatia.
400 B.C.E.	First Greek colonies appear on islands in the Adriatic Sea.
100 B.C.E.– 400 A.D.	Croatia is part of the Roman Empire.
Early 600s	Slavic tribes including Croats settle in Croatia.
ca. 800	Appearance of first Croatian dukes, or warlords
910–928	Tomislav wins over Hungarians and Bulgarians and expands the country.
925–1089	Trpimirovic dynasty rules.
1102	Beginning of Croatian-Hungarian kingdom.
1242	Mongolian invasion of the kingdom.
1526	Battle of Mohac and death of King Louis.
1527	Nobles ask the ruling family of Austria, the Habsburgs, to rule over Croatia.
1553	The Military Border is formed to help defend Croatia.
18th century	Age of absolutism and Germanization of Croatia.
1797	French forces occupy Croatia and form Illyrian provinces, including Dubrovnik.
1868	Croatian signs an agreement with Hungary and gains limited control over its internal affairs.
1914–1918	Croatia participates in World War I.
1918	Kingdom of Serbs, Croats, and Slovenians established and organized on democratic principles.
1928	Assassination of Croatian political leaders at Parliament meeting in Belgrade.
1929	King Karadjordjevic dismisses Parliament and proclaims a dictatorship in Yugoslavia.
1939	Croatia receives greater autonomy in Yugoslavia after an agreement between Serbian and Croatian leaders.
1941	German occupation of Yugoslavia. Croatian extremists declare independent country.
1945	End of World War II. Croatia again part of Yugoslavia.

1990	Democratic elections. Franjo Tudjman becomes first president.
1991	After referendum, Croatia declares independence from Yugoslavia.
1991–1995	Armed conflict between Croats and Serbs.
1992	Croatia becomes member of the United Nations.
1995	Tudjman reelected president.
2000	Opposition wins parliamentary and presidential elections. Stipe Mesic elected president. Croatia becomes member of the World Trade Organization.

Further Reading

Bilus, Ivanka, et al. *Croatia at the Table: The Aromas and Tastes of Croatian Cuisine.* Alfa, 1997.

Goldstein, Ivo   Nikolina Jovanovic (Trans.). *Croatia: A History.* McGill-Queens University Press, 1999.

Naprijed, Naklada. *The Croatian Adriatic: Features of Cultural and Natural Interest.* Seven Hills Book Distributor, 1999.

Oliver, Jeanne. *Lonely Planet Croatia.* Lonely Planet Publications, 2002.

Croatia: Explore the World. Nelles Verlag, 1998.

Index

Index

About the Author

ZORAN "ZOK" PAVLOVIĆ is a graduate student in geography at South Dakota State University, Brookings, where he is pursuing his passion for learning about the world's people and places. Zok was born and raised in Croatia. He is a devoted gourmet cook and wine enthusiast, passions that he shares with his wife, Erin, and his mentor and fellow connoisseur, Charles F. "Fritz" Gritzner.

CHARLES F. "FRITZ" GRITZNER is Distinguished Professor of Geography at South Dakota State University. He is now in his fifth decade of college teaching and research. Much of his career work has focused on geographic education. Fritz has served as both president and executive director of the National Council for Geographic Education and has received the Council's George J. Miller Award for Distinguished Service.